RICH
– WHO CARES?

RICHIE
Who Cares?

Richie Barlow
with Becky Bond

Scratching Shed Publishing Ltd

Cover photography: © Alex Wightman
Back cover: Richie today; a hug from Mamma Pauline;
and meeting Ben at Betty's, in Harrogate, June 2014

A catalogue record for this book is available
from the British Library.

Typeset in Adobe Caslon Pro
Printed and bound in the United Kingdom by

Short Run Press Ltd
Bittern Road, Sowton Industrial Estate, Exeter. EX2 7LW
Tel: 01392 211909   Fax: 01392 444134

To those who, by the failures of adults and authorities, didn't make it to tell their truths

Contents

Richie's birthday, 1995. Mamma Pauline is getting angry at Brett (*out of shot*), who came into the room racially abusing her, trying to spoil the party

•

Acknowledgements

THERE ARE some key people in my life without whose support and interventions I would not be here today. They were flickers of hope in my darkest and most desperate times and I cannot thank them enough for the kindness they showed me when others could not have cared less.

In the process of writing this book, some of them have shared background stories about the care system they worked in. Things that, as a child, I could never have known or understood. That system was broken in so many ways that a whole other tome could be written about it. It was riddled with racist, sexist and homophobic staff on poor wages in vastly under-resourced circumstances. That is no excuse. Those supposed care-givers were adults who had a choice and I was a child who did not.

I hope I have conveyed the compassion and love of those who really did have my best interests at heart throughout this story. I think it speaks volumes that many of them are still in my adult life, involving me in their own families and sharing in my hard-fought quest for happiness.

From Willowdene, Jill and Christine.

From Farmlands, Gary, Rose and Avril. And Tim, who was my only friend there.

My link worker, Pauline (Mamma), who still has my goldfish bowl in her garage.

My foster mum, Anna Daiches, whom I hope will one day be my actual mum.

Richie – Who Cares?

My Guardian Angel in life after the care system, Richard.

The Truth Project, for believing me and steering me towards help and justice.

My Solicitor, Debbie, for all her hard work to find my records and act on the truth held within them.

My Counsellor, Alexandra, for listening and letting me unload.

The artists whose music helped me switch off and find solace in times of crisis – Madonna and Alison Moyet.

The actor Anthony Rapp, whose honesty and bravery gave me the courage and inspiration to share my own story.

From *Star Trek*, Gene and Majel Roddenberry, whose creation inspired, educated and was integral to my development.

My ghostwriter Becky Bond, who asked hundreds of questions and helped me put my words in order and shaped this book.

My publisher Phil Caplan at Scratching Shed Publishing, for treating my story with the care and attention it deserves.

My friend Niall, for his kind support and his gold-standard humour.

My Press and Publicity Manager, Sofia Cann from Cann Communications, who worked tirelessly to give my story its rightful recognition.

And of course, my husband Ben, who understands me completely and loves me regardless.

Thank you.

Foreword

•

Niall Paterson

I AM one of the lucky ones.

My childhood was not without its ups and downs, of course. Skinned knees, bullies, broken hearts. But every time I fell, my mum and dad were there to pick me up.

Our home was warm, literally and figuratively. Love was as abundant as food. My brother and I lacked neither, and we took for granted the attention and care that my parents lavished upon us.

Mum and dad treated us this way because well – that's just what parents do.

The realisation that many parents don't – that instead of care and attention, thousands of children are gifted little more than torture and anguish – came to me late.

Yes, there were always those hushed comments about the state of someone's uniform; or if they hadn't been to school for days and when they did they carried bruises or just a desire to sit in a corner. But did I genuinely believe that any of my contemporaries were being abused by their parents?

I was not a naive young adult; I read widely, was already obsessed with the news – I knew evil existed, but almost entirely as an abstraction.

Richie – Who Cares?

A lifetime of reporting at home and abroad, of witnessing first hand the depths to which humanity can sink and still plummet further, disabused me of that.

The bodies in Afghanistan, charred and twisted, the faces locked forever in forced grins as their skin burned.

The terrorist attacks and genuine fear in the voices of those caught up in them, yet still defiant enough to want to speak about what they saw.

And particularly that afternoon spent listening in family court to police reports, detailing in dispassionate terms, the most gruesome abuse imaginable on a three-year-old.

For some people, exposure to the dirt under society's fingernails spurs them into action. For me, and many of my journalistic contemporaries, the years spent in pursuit of the news have served to somewhat numb the extremities.

Entirely natural, of course. The job would be impossible otherwise.

Yet I am not embarrassed to admit that what follows in this book has affected me as much as anything ever could.

Richie and his husband Ben are the most wonderful couple you could imagine. On our first meeting, my son and I strolled through a balmy Soho only to encounter two big, bluff, joyous lads grinning from ear to ear but sweating buckets, having struggled to carry a huge, gift-wrapped present halfway across London, on the tube, in the heat.

The wee man fell in love with them that day, and so did I.

So to read what my friend has been brave enough to admit to and strong enough to endure has reminded me that, whilst there are times to be dispassionate, to park one's emotions, perhaps we should not do so in the face of the abuse of the defenceless.

Most abuse happens not at the hands of the faceless predator with an unmarked van, but by people known to the victim, often their own family.

Odds are you'll have encountered an abuser. Odds are higher you'll know someone abused.

Yet where is the anger?

Sure, we all reach for the hashtags when another story of abuse comes to dominate the news cycle. But do we genuinely recognise that these are but the iceberg's tip, that every hour of every day someone not far from you is closing their eyes and praying for their grave?

But there is hope. Even in this book, large parts of which could best be characterised by the hopelessness that Richie felt for so much of his life.

For every time that someone tells their story, unvarnished and without filter, there is a chance we edge a little closer to a world in which we all know the signs and are unafraid to act on them.

I don't know if Richie and Ben want children; I do know if they did they would devote themselves to being the kind of parents that I had, and took so much for granted.

I am proud to know Richie, and even prouder to call him my friend. This is his story.

Niall Paterson
Sky News

Richie

1

•

An Accident

YOU PROBABLY shouldn't be reading this. As this memoir comes out, I'm on the cusp of my fortieth birthday. How, I have no idea.

Nottingham, 1988

'You tell 'em you fell down the stairs, right?'

I knew better than to speak the truth. It would have been more than my life was worth. I'd seen what she was capable of, been at the hands of her abuse for as long as I could remember. But this was different. This time, somebody else witnessed my mother's wrath and called 999.

'Yes,' I nodded, wiping salt-washed blood from my teary eyes.

Blue lights flashed through the galley kitchen window, the siren silenced before pulling into our Nottinghamshire council estate. I could hear the ambulance doors opening and closing, footsteps moving quickly towards the back door. Aged just six, I sensed my mother's panic as she roughly mopped my face with a tea-towel and tried to stem the red river from my blond hair.

'It's your own fault,' she hissed in my ear.

My head was pounding, I felt dizzy and sore all over, but my physical pain was nothing compared to how I felt inside.

Pulling her own greasy mop into a dirty bobble, she smoothed her skirt and plastered on a concerned face. A transformation back to Dr Jekyll from Mrs Hyde, which I was only too familiar with; her public persona of a loving, doting parent masking the horror of what was happening behind closed – and locked – doors.

Events leading up to this moment had been innocent enough, as they usually were. I'd spent the day with a nice lady called Karen while my mother worked her shift on the frozen food stall in the market. I liked going to Karen's because I was allowed to have lunch. She even let me play outside or watch television, which I never got to do at home. So perhaps, when my mother came to pick me up, I just looked too damn happy for her liking, and she wanted to knock that smile off my face.

After the usual 'hello' and 'has he been behaving himself?' my mother told Karen she'd like a word with me in private before we set off home. 'Here, take a cig and go for a smoke in the garden,' she suggested.

'Alright Catherine, cheers,' Karen said, picking up the packet and matches, 'I'll be out the back.'

As soon as Karen shut the door, my mother's eyes narrowed as she leaned in to whisper that I was going to get it for being such a deviant. I felt sick. I didn't know what was coming but I knew it was going to hurt.

Digging her nails into my arm, she yanked me into the hallway, pulled my pants down and threw me over her knee on the chair at the bottom of the stairs and began hitting me harder and harder. Tears were stinging the corners of my eyes as each blow threw my head closer to the lip of the splintered wooden staircase.

I couldn't understand what I'd done this time. Why was she hitting me? Had Karen told her I'd been naughty? Had I looked at her wrong again? I didn't think so. I was a good boy. I'd been good. I yelped as my forehead crashed into the hard step. Winded, I tried to catch my breath, but before I had chance – *slam* – it happened again. I screwed my eyes shut, trying to pretend it wasn't happening, but a sob escaped.

'Stop crying,' she spat, increasing the weight and speed of her blows. The pain in my head was splitting, overtaking the burning slaps across my backside and legs. I clenched my jaw to stop the scream. If I made any more noise, there'd be much worse to come at home. She was lost in a frenzy of anger, pounding out her frustration into her youngest son's tiny body.

Then the sound of the back door opening brought the abuse to a sudden halt. Pulling my pants back up in one swift move, she twisted me around and made out she'd just caught me at the bottom of the stairs. Karen stepped into the hallway and saw my bleeding head and semi-concussion.

'Oh my God, what's happened?' she screamed.

'He fell down your stairs Karen. Went up for a wee before we set off and took a right tumble. Are you alright, love?' my mother cooed at me. I could barely speak with the shock and pain, still struggling to catch my breath.

'Look at his head, Catherine. It's pouring with blood, I'll fetch a tea-towel.' I put my hand to my forehead and felt the slick liquid running between my fingers.

'It looks bad, Catherine. I'm calling an ambulance.'

She darted into the kitchen and grabbed a tea-towel to give to my mother, then ran to the house phone on the hall table and dialled the emergency services. My mother put me down on the bottom step and faced me, her back to Karen.

'You're so clumsy, aren't you?' my mother sneered, harshly rubbing my wound.

'Yes,' I nodded, my priority being to avoid any more pain.

Something in the way Karen looked over at me suggested she didn't believe my mother. I sensed she was uneasy with the situation. Speaking to the lady on the phone she said she hadn't seen it happen, but my mother *told her* I'd tripped at the top of the stairs and fallen. Karen seemed to want to come over and shield me, I felt she understood, silently willing me to tell the truth. But that was never going to happen.

'They're on their way,' she said, hanging up.

As we waited for the ambulance to arrive, my mother made such a fuss of me in front of Karen that I almost believed she hadn't meant to hit me. I always wished she'd be sorry, to say she'd never do it again, it was an accident and that she loved me, but those words

3

remained unspoken. I sat there, numb and woozy, wondering what was going to happen to me when I got home for causing such a fuss.

I was too young to remember what the paramedics said to me, or if they pushed the issue privately with Karen. They must have seen all sorts. But I *do* know that even if a friendly face had taken me to one side and tried to tease the truth out of me, I wouldn't have told. My mother's mental grip on me was powerful. She was capable of anything.

I was bandaged up and given gentle warnings about making sure my laces were tied properly next time, and to watch where I was going. Then the paramedics got back in the ambulance and drove off. Karen reached into the biscuit tin and gave me a bourbon to eat on the way home, which I squirreled away in my pocket.

'You take care now,' she said, kneeling in front of me, eyes clocking the hand-sized welts forming on the side of my calves.

'Thanks so much Karen,' my mother purred, 'You're a real angel. I can't believe he fell all the way down.'

'Me neither,' she said flatly.

Taking my hand, my mother continued to play the part of a loving parent, until we were round the corner and out of sight.

'And you can give me that biscuit too, you little deviant.'

I'M THE middle child of three. My big brother, Luke, is roughly eighteen months older and my little sister, Claire, a similar gap younger. But it was me who received most of the abuse, until my stepdad moved in and took it to another level.

The catastrophic domino effect began when I was about four. Some of the dates are sketchy because the level of trauma was such that, psychologists say, people like me blank things out to cope.

What I know for sure though, is that it was my mother's cruelty in my primary years which ultimately led me to a childhood in the care system, where, among other horrors, I was forced into prostitution, aged just nine.

2

•

Fish Fingers

FROM THE outside, our council house looked like all the others in the area – run down and unloved, like me. But nobody could have imagined what it was like inside my bedroom.

My sister Claire's room was beautiful, situated at the front and right opposite mine. She had pink carpet and lace curtains. She had a lightbulb with a lightshade and proper bedding. She had a wardrobe with pretty dresses in and lots of toys, which she was allowed to play with whenever she liked. Her door handle hadn't been tampered with.

I shared a room with Luke. My mother had doctored our handle so we couldn't get out unless she wanted us to. It was one of those with a square metal rod through it, so if you didn't have the rod, you couldn't open the door from the inside. To be sure though, she'd fixed a bolt at the top, almost out of sight.

There were two beds, with one single itchy blanket each, covering bare mattresses, sat on top of rough floorboards. No pillows, no curtains, and the worn catches on the dirty windows were also broken – jammed shut and snapped off so that no fresh air could get in and we couldn't get out. In the winter, it was freezing because there was no heating. When it was dark, we couldn't see anything because we didn't have a lightbulb, let alone a shade. There was one scruffy bedside cabinet between us and a locked wardrobe.

If we were going to be shut in for a few days, she sometimes left us a potty but often she didn't bother. When tummy ache and desperation took over, we had to go to the toilet in the corner of the room or in a drawer on top of clothes so that it wouldn't seep through the floor. When she saw what we'd done, we'd be punished. We couldn't eat or drink until she decided to let us out.

It was so unfair. We couldn't understand why Claire had such a nice bedroom and could come and go freely, yet we had nothing. We were so envious of the way she was treated. Why would our mother do that? What had we done to deserve this treatment? The only reason we could see was that we were boys.

At least when Luke was locked in with me, we had each other for company, even though we were starving. But more often than not, I was alone because my mother reserved a particular vitriol for me. Looking back, I think she sensed I was different – knew that I wasn't going to be the son she expected.

The reasons for being incarcerated were wide-ranging but always random. It could be anything from holding a spoon wrongly, to daring to look longingly at the food on her plate or asking for something in a way she perceived to be an incorrect tone. I lived on eggshells, always dreading the next round of punishments because although being locked in a room without food, light, warmth or a potty was bad, it was far from the worst weapon in her arsenal.

Luke was braver. He used to plot our escape. He'd think of ways to break through the window and tie bedsheets to scale down the wall. We'd dream up fantasies of flying through the glass, up over and out of the estate to somewhere better with kind parents who loved us and took us places. We tried to imagine how it would feel to open a fridge full of food and be allowed to eat anything, or go to school without holes in our shoes and have friends.

When we were locked in, we didn't exist to our mother. Her life carried on as normal. I'd hear her talking to Claire or listening to the radio, acting as if nothing was wrong. I've no idea what Claire thought at the time, she was so young, but she probably felt lucky not to be stuck in a room. Once our stepdad came on the scene though, I'm sure she'd rather have been barricaded away.

Sometimes, the aroma of cooking drifted upstairs and that was particularly hard to cope with, knowing we weren't going to be getting any of it. Once, she made fish fingers and chips for Claire's lunch after we'd been locked in for two days. Our stomachs were beyond growling, we were weak with hunger and thirst. It was literally torture. We began wondering what there might be in the room that we could eat, just to put something in our tummies.

Luke had an idea. 'We wait until she goes out and then we burrow through the door,' he said.

It sounded mad, but by then I was willing to try anything. We began looking at the door closely – but quietly, until we felt sure, hours later, that she'd left the house. It was very flimsy, just two thin pieces of veneer, packed in the middle with corrugated cardboard. Luke thought if we could peel back the veneers, we might be able to squeeze through and steal some fishfingers from the freezer.

Together, using what fingernails we had, we gradually scratched and chipped away at the bottom corner, but it was hard to get the right angle with it being closed. With persistence and sheer desperation on our side though, we somehow managed to hook our fingers under a tiny bit of the edge and gently pull.

'It's working,' Luke said.

'I'm scared. What if she finds out? She'll kill us.'

'Do you want something to eat or not?'

We carried on, trying our hardest to prise the veneer away from the corner of the door. I wedged my tiny hand in and teased out some shreds of cardboard. Before I had chance to register what I was doing, I began stuffing pieces of the dusty cardboard into my mouth, my stomach so desperate to consume anything.

Luke's shocked look soon changed as he followed my lead, sliding his hand further up to reach more shreds. It tasted disgusting – dry and hard with no liquid to swill it down. But it was cardboard or nothing. We were young boys, trapped in a room with no idea when we'd be let out.

We didn't know if our mother was at work or had nipped to the shops, so after nearly choking on the door padding, we moved fast, spurred by the prospect of real food downstairs in the kitchen.

I was smaller than Luke, so rather than try and make the hole bigger for both of us to get out, Luke said I should go on my own as fast as I could, then run back with the fish fingers. That way, we could eat them in the bedroom without her knowing.

I reached in again and pushed the other side, which seemed to pop open more easily. Crawling out on my stomach, I used my elbows for purchase on the carpet at the other side, and like a commando, breathed in to make myself as long and thin as possible to squeeze through. I knew I mustn't damage the door - it had to look untouched. I grazed all my stomach and sides, but barely registered the pain. Then once through, I stayed low and still and silent for about thirty seconds, just to check she hadn't come back. It was a massive risk.

'Hurry up. Run,' said Luke.

I slid all the way down the stairs and went straight to the freezer, pulling at drawers, desperate for a morsel of anything. Third drawer down, they were there. I knew better than to take the whole box, so shook out a fistful, threw the box back in the drawer, slammed the door shut and pelted back upstairs, stuffing one in my mouth, dropping a few breadcrumbs along the way. When I got to the top of the stairs, I tried to ease back the veneer again, with Luke pushing from the inside too. Panic was rising fast.

'Pass the fish fingers,' he yelled in desperation.

'I'm trying, hang on.' I shoved them through and Luke stuffed one into his mouth while holding the other side of the door back. I hefted myself back through about halfway, then Luke grabbed my wrists and dragged the rest of my torso through.

Jubilant, we both leaned back against the door and began to gnaw at the solid rations, sucking out any moisture we could. In all the hurry, I hadn't had time to get us a drink. Not dared to.

It was pitiful. We can't have had more than five fishfingers between us. I doubt they were even nutritious. She wouldn't waste her money on quality brands, opting for the cheapest junk to ensure she had enough cash left for her booze and drugs. When we were let out the next day, she didn't say anything about the door or the missing food. I thought we'd got away with it.

About a week later, she presented me with a plate piled high with frozen fish fingers, which I had to eat in front of her as punishment for stealing. She never mentioned the bedroom door and must have assumed I'd taken them when it wasn't locked.

They were disgusting to eat when I was starving but forcing down a whole packet when I wasn't hungry was worse. Even when I started vomiting, she made me continue until I'd swallowed every last bite. My tummy hurt so much. It didn't occur to her that Luke might have played a part in the theft too, but I didn't tell on him. He was the only friend I had.

Shortly after that, she put a padlock on the freezer.

My mother's need to control what and when we ate was a dominant part of her abuse. We would be starved for three days, then made to eat gigantic portions at the table with her, knowing our tiny bellies would be in agony after so long without food. If we looked at her plate, she'd make us eat hers too.

This bizarre relationship with food manifested itself in my behaviour at the first children's home I was sent to. I'd always ask for more than I needed, then leave a lot. A fast-feast mentality had become entrenched in my psyche.

Her use of chilli powder as a punishment also had an adverse effect on me later in life. I'm now so allergic to it that even the slightest sprinkle in a meal leaves me covered in blisters. It was her favourite and most regular form of abuse, even more popular than squeezing washing up liquid down my throat, which happened for the first time after a wrestling match on television.

I'd been taken to the house next door for some reason. I considered myself lucky because the alternative was being locked in my bedroom. In the neighbour's lounge sat four older men, all glued to the TV, so I found a space on the floor and watched with them.

I'd never seen wrestling before, so just followed the lead of the men, shouting and cheering whenever they did. I loved the drama of it, the costumes, the showmanship. It was so colourful and exciting. The wrestlers all had special names which we yelled out as the rounds continued. One of them was called Ship Boat.

When my mother came back, she heard me chanting 'Ship Boat, Ship Boat, Ship Boat' but she thought I was swearing, saying 'Shit Boat'.

Her eyes narrowed and she started shouting at me for my bad language, slapping me over the head. The men didn't stick up for me. Stupidly, I made the mistake of answering her back.

'It's not a rude word,' I said.

'Pardon?'

'I said SHIP Boat. The wrestler's called SHIP boat.'

She grabbed me by the wrist and hauled me out of the room, dragging me home. It was humiliating being told off in front of those men, but I think they knew better than to interfere. They were probably too drunk to be bothered with another domestic.

She pushed me through the kitchen door and pinned me against the unit as her eyes darted around, wondering what she was going to feed me with this time – chilli powder, soap or washing-up liquid? The latter was closest, so she forced my head back and my mouth open and as I screamed, she squirted it directly down my throat. She was a woman on a mission.

Immediately, my stomach heaved as greasy chemicals bubbled and burned. I could feel it all around my teeth and tongue, slimy and gritty and poisonous. It felt like my throat was being destroyed, it was so painful I could barely breathe or speak. She grabbed the back of my head and pushed my face to the sink to vomit, but I was too small to reach over and clattered my chin on the edge.

She was poisoning me. My own mother, who was meant to be caring and loving was terrorising me for something I hadn't even done wrong. But I'd learned I shouldn't cry. I mustn't. If I did, she might force more down my throat or reach for the chilli powder, which was even worse. I felt sad and confused and very, very sick.

Only when there was nothing left for me to throw up, did she make me swill my mouth out with water. But this wasn't to get rid of the taste for me, it was to get rid of the evidence for her. It took forever. Every time I took a sip, my body rejected it. Eventually, she tired of the rigmarole, marched me upstairs and locked me in.

Covered in my own vomit and fighting back tears, I wondered what I had ever done to deserve this life. All I wanted was to be part of a normal family, where I was looked after, cared for, fed and loved.

3

•

Chilli Powder

I DON'T remember my dad leaving.

He was in the background one minute, then somehow, I just realised he wasn't there anymore. That's when my mother started having a lot of parties, which often went on all weekend and involved many men. I was always locked in my bedroom for these events without food, water, toys or toilet facilities. My only comfort was hearing music thumping through the floor. But there was one thing she couldn't control – and that was my imagination.

She played a lot of Meatloaf and Bon Jovi which I really didn't like, but occasionally, Madonna came on. I fell in love with Madonna's music after watching 'Like A Prayer' on video through a crack in the lounge door. Whenever I heard the intro after that, I mentally transported myself into the scene.

Laid on my cold bed, I'd picture myself as the black Jesus behind bars in church, needing to escape. I wondered how it would feel for someone to look at me the way Madonna looked at him. More than anything else in the world, I wanted to be loved. This was my coping mechanism to block everything else out but when my brain tired, I picked the paint off the windowsill, knowing there'd be trouble later.

Fantasies saved me, but sometimes they spilled over into hallucinations, most likely induced by hunger. I vividly remember once seeing a plate of hot buttered toast, teetering at the side of my bed. I reached down to grab a slice and felt the crunch of perfectly browned pieces lathered in melted butter, dripping all over my lips. I licked my fingers after finishing it, feeling full and content. When I came to, I was so convinced I'd eaten it that I scoured my room for the plate. But of course, nothing. I was still starving. She'd probably left some outside the bedroom door for me to smell but not eat.

During her parties, boredom would sometimes be broken by the sound of people going to the toilet next to my room. Another kick in the teeth. Everyone else could use the bathroom except me. I'd hear each little movement and splash and eventually got to the stage where I could tell when it was her boyfriend Neil.

The locked wardrobe in my bedroom always tempted me. I never dared ask what was inside, but my curiosity built and built over the long hours and days I'd stared at it. What was in there? Was she hiding something important? Could there be food? It must be something interesting, I reasoned, if it had to be kept locked.

Inevitably, one Saturday night I gave in to temptation and tried to break in. I thought nobody would hear above the music, so after casting around the room for some kind of tool, I pulled off a rough splinter from under the windowsill. The wood can't have been more than three centimetres long and only a few millimetres thick. I thought if I slid the splinter into the crack of the door and moved it upwards, it might release it.

To my astonishment, it worked and was much easier than I'd expected. I wondered why I hadn't tried before, but knew deep down it was fear preventing me, the terror of being caught snooping. It crossed my mind that she might have even locked the wardrobe as a test, knowing I'd eventually crumble.

With ears on high alert, I slowly and gently pulled the wardrobe door back and peaked around the edge. There were piles of carboard boxes, haphazardly thrown in, a broken radio, electrical wires, damaged cassette tapes and an open margarine tub holding various sized rusting batteries. Junk. The sort of stuff you keep, to deal with another time. To me, it was a treasure trove.

Sandwiched between the boxes were some of her old clothes. Instinctively, I buried my nose into one of the jumpers, hoping for a whiff of comfort, but her scent only conjoured dread so I threw it back inside, heart racing.

It felt like a warning.

Gingerly picking through, I came across piles of old paperwork which I couldn't make sense of. I was no good at reading because my mother didn't send me to school regularly, preferring to keep me hidden away in case anyone noticed tell-tale bruising. I thought some of the letters looked official, because they were on headed paper, but they could have been anything – unpaid bills, divorce proceedings from my dad, unreturned slips for school trips.

Right at the back, I spotted two of my toy cars. One of them was similar to a real car my dad had – a Ford Capri, and the other was a blue and white police car with a wheel missing. They kept me entertained for hours as I pretended I was being rescued and they were arriving at the house, sending everyone at the party away. They were making my mother say sorry for everything she'd done, and she hugged me, and I felt safe.

When the music stopped and people were leaving, I knew I had to put everything back quickly, even though I desperately wanted to hide some things under my mattress for next time. But re-stacking the boxes was a lot harder than taking them out, and I couldn't remember where everything went. Bits kept tumbling back out, then the door wouldn't close properly. I didn't know how to re-lock it from the outside. What was I going to do?

I could hear my mother's footsteps coming up the stairs and I shivered. If she saw, I'd be dead. I leaned against the wardrobe door to keep it shut and prayed that for once, she wouldn't be thinking of releasing me. I'd rather have another two days of starvation than deal with the consequences of this transgression.

She stopped on the landing, and I could sense her hovering at the other side, intoxicated, wondering if I was worth the bother. Screwing my eyes shut, I willed her to keep walking to her bedroom. Even listening to her and Neil making noises in there was preferable.

I got a reprieve.

Or so I thought.

Richie – Who Cares?

The relief of her not coming in made my whole body relax and somehow, I eventually fell asleep, slumped against the wardrobe door. Next thing I knew, she was towering above me as I came to. A few boxes lay beside me having spilled out in the night and her hot breath was in my face.

'What. Have. You. Done?' she menaced.

I thought I was going to wet myself with fear. I knew I was getting the chilli powder.

'I'm sorry, I didn't mean to, it was open. I'm sorry mum, please don't do it,' I begged 'please.'

Dragging me down the stairs she pulled me into the kitchen and threw me up against the corner of the units, pushing her body against mine so I couldn't escape. I could barely breathe from the pressure of her, the utter panic of knowing what was coming. A look of pure evil spread across her face as she reached up to the top cupboard for her catering-sized jar of chilli powder. She pulled it down and unscrewed the lid, eyes boring into mine. Grabbing a dirty tablespoon from the countertop, she drove it into the jar.

'Open up,' she said.

'Please mum, no, I'm sorry, I didn't mean it, I won't do it again,' I sobbed.

'I said, *open up.*'

I just couldn't. I knew how painful it was going to be. I'd felt that searing heat shoot through my veins so many times, and each time it got worse.

With her other hand, she squeezed my jaw with such force that I yelled in pain, at which point she quickly rammed the whole spoonful in and out of my mouth, depositing the chilli there. Then letting the spoon clatter to the floor, she forced my jaw up, holding the top of my head to keep it closed, like a vice.

I could barely breathe, my eyes wide with fear as I felt the rising temperature burning my gums, my mouth, my lips and all down the back of my throat.

'Swallow it.'

It was too dry. I couldn't. Not one fibre in my body could tolerate any more heat. The powder reached my nose and burned into my sinuses. I began choking, the chilli catching in my lungs, making my little body convulse.

Her favourite abuse.

'Swallow it,' she repeated.

I tried, through sheer terror, to swallow some of the powder. The sooner I did it, the sooner I'd be able to breathe again. It was suffocate or swallow.

'You are a deviant. This is what you deserve. This is what happens when you defy me.'

My skin and insides were raw with heat. I knew I couldn't tolerate any more. She saw I was on the brink and released my jaw, shoving my face into the sink where I began to vomit. But as the powder came back up, mixed with bile, the pain increased. It felt like I was spewing boiling water.

Forcing my head under the cold tap, she made me gulp as much as I could – swilling my mouth and spitting, then swallowing more water. It made no difference. Even the water felt hot. All the while she was telling me that it was my own fault, that I shouldn't have opened the wardrobe.

When she tired, I was dragged back up to my room, where she snatched up my toy cars and re-locked the wardrobe, making me stand and stare at it.

'Next time, it'll be worse' she said, slamming and locking the door behind her.

I was in agony for hours. There was nothing I could do but wait. She'd left me with burning insides and no water. I tried to think of anything to take the pain away and, eyes streaming, I forced my mind back to the one happy memory I had of a coach holiday to Blackpool when my grandma and grandad came.

My grandparents loved it there. Grandma was Blackpool mad, her house covered in trinkets from the many gift shops on the promenade – miniature towers, snowstorms, thimbles, the lot. Her lounge featured glass cabinets chockablock full of tat. Her own private Aladdin's Cave.

The coach trip was so exciting. I couldn't believe there was a television at the front playing Madonna videos. I didn't know what

Richie – Who Cares?

I wanted to do more, watch the dancers on screen or look out of the window. It was such a novelty to be going somewhere, seeing something different, sat near new people.

The main reason I enjoyed that holiday though was because my mother wasn't abusive when we were in company. She had her nice face on and I could almost pretend she was like that all the time. The devil was always lurking under the surface though, ready to pounce should I dare to suggest anything as bold as taking our sandals off to paddle.

But, for a short time, I felt safer.

The best bit of that trip, the part I was trying my hardest to recall, to soothe my blistering mouth, was a visit to a new ice cream parlour. We were the very first customers and were offered all you can eat ice-cream, then had our photograph taken for the local newspaper. I felt like royalty.

It was the cold, sweet taste of mint choc chip that I wanted to remember now, to block out the pain.

About a year after the Blackpool coach holiday, my mother met her new husband-to-be, a paedophile.

4

•

Dual Threat

FOR A VERY short time, things were better. My mother seemed happy with her new boyfriend, so the punishments became less frequent. Until he moved in.

I was seven and the only way to explain how I felt about that is evil seeping through the cracks. The dynamics changed overnight, and everything got even darker. The mask he'd been wearing to woo my mother slipped, revealing his twisted temperament.

Before he'd even laid a finger on me, I sensed his underlying aggression. And as he witnessed my mother's abuse creeping back in, he assumed he had a green light to mirror that – and more, marking his territory like a rabid dog.

The first time he tried to discipline me, my mother was out. I'd had the audacity to go looking for a slice of bread in the kitchen. But I'd been noisy, banging the lid of the bread bin too hard. I looked up to see him leaning against the door frame, staring at me.

'There's nothing in there for you,' he said.

'I'm hungry,' I replied.

'Didn't you hear me? I said there's nothing in there *for you*.'

'You're not my dad. You can't tell me what to do.'

He wore a black, two-rowed studded belt threaded through frost wash jeans. It was the kind of belt a punk might wear, the sort of thing that wouldn't look out of place around a scary dog's neck. His face snarled with rising anger, edging closer towards me.

'What did you say?'

'Nothing. I didn't say anything,' I replied quietly, looking at the floor.

'Don't lie to me. I heard you say something, what was it?' he growled, unbuckling his belt and slowly pulling it out of the loopholes.

'Nothing. It was nothing,' I said.

His fingers were caressing the soft leather and hard studs.

'Because, I thought you said *you're not my dad*.'

I knew I was in for it. He put the ends of the belt together to form a loop and snapped them, hard, in front of my face. I could see his jaw clenching and a small vein pulsing in his neck. His stale breath filled my nostrils, and I turned my face from his jutting jaw.

'Is that right?' he said.

I started trembling and crying as he snapped his belt next to my ear again and again, daring me to challenge him one more time.

'I don't know. I don't know what I said,' my voice trembling.

He raised his right arm like he was about to bowl but came down on me with the studded belt in a shocking series of blows, thrashing me wherever he could – legs, arms, backside and when I dared to look up through my arms – my face. He was possessed. The pain was brutal. I'd never been beaten by the full force of a man before. My real dad never hit me.

'Stop. Please stop,' I sobbed.

But he wasn't satisfied until I was cowering in a corner, trying to cover my fresh welts which were rapidly forming all across my neck, knuckles and back. I was crying my eyes out to the point where I could barely breathe.

Then my mother walked in. Thank God, I thought, she'll stop him. She'll tell him not to do it again. But she surveyed the scene of her youngest boy, battered and bloodied, tears streaking out of his blue eyes and smiled at Tony.

'*He's* your dad now,' she said, 'we're getting married.'

I was locked in my room again for disobeying her new fiancé.

But for everything he did to me – it was nothing compared to the pain he inflicted on Claire. He hated Luke and I, but he lusted over our little sister.

On my mother and Tony's wedding day, Luke, Claire and myself got to wear new clothes. She wanted to present us as a normal, functioning family and I was happy to pretend because with other people around, she couldn't hurt me. I hated and feared Tony, and absolutely didn't want her to marry him but there was no point protesting, so I decided to make the most of a day out of the house, hoping to see Grandma and Grandad too.

The ceremony still remains a bit of a blur but I believe it was in Nottingham registry office. The reception was in a local pub, about as basic as you could get in the late '80s - sticky carpets and reeking of cigarette smoke. But I felt free, running in between all the guests, helping myself to sausage rolls and crisps from the buffet. I knew I'd be in trouble later, but it was worth it in the moment.

Everyone was getting drunk as the music grew louder. The difference this time was that for once, I wasn't locked away from it all. I could even go to a proper toilet and was allowed to play with my little sister Claire. I filled myself full of food and reveled in the company because I never knew when I might get to eat or talk to people again.

They didn't have a honeymoon so there was no chance of respite and, only a few days later, a new abuse was introduced. One they could both enjoy. It was locking me in the cupboard under the stairs. The reasons for this punishment were just as vague – a wrong look, a request for a drink, a word spoken incorrectly. Sometimes, they put me in there just because they didn't want to look at me.

It was the summer holidays and baking hot inside and out. I'd been offered the rare opportunity to play outside with Luke and grasped it with both hands. It was busy on our estate with other kids playing and neighbours sat on their front steps, making the most of the sunshine. We didn't have the luxury of owning a football or bike, so we were just messing around, playing hide and seek. Luke ran off to hide and I had my hands over my eyes, peeking through to see where he was going, counting to twenty.

'Coming ready or not,' I shouted.

I began running around the estate, calling his name, searching for him behind garden fences, seeing if he was crouching next to the bins or over by the bus stop. 'He's not here, lovey,' one of the elderly residents said, looking up from her magazine.

'Luke, where are you?' I yelled.

I caught a glimpse of him darting down a little alleyway towards the park, so set off running in that direction. But I wasn't looking where my feet were going and stumbled over a loose pavement slab, losing my balance and falling flat on my face. The graze on my cheek stung like mad, but worse was my knee, which I'd cut open on a tiny piece of glass. The blood began dripping down my shin and I tried to stem it with my fingers, picking out the shard and chucking it back on the ground.

'Luke!' I yelled, 'I've fallen.' But he didn't come. Maybe he hadn't heard me or perhaps he'd used this opportunity to run back to our real dad's house. Despite having fallen, I wanted to stay out and play for longer, but with no Luke and my knee really beginning to hurt, I hobbled home on my own.

I wasn't expecting sympathy, but I'd hoped for a plaster to stop the bleeding. How foolish. Tony's face said it all. My crying and bloody knee had ruined his few minutes of peace, he told me. What was he going to do now, he wondered?

My eyes quickly flicked to his waist and as I saw the studded belt, instantly felt trembly again. But his hand went to his pocket instead of his buckle, and, turning towards the under-stair cupboard, I noticed the corners of his mouth twitching upwards.

'Get in there,' he said. I followed his gaze and thought he must be wrong. Why would I get into a cupboard? Would there be any room? 'Get. In.' he repeated, moving towards me.

I had no option. It was that or the belt and I couldn't take the belt again – especially on top of my freshly cut knee and grazed face.

He moved over to the cupboard door and kicked it wide open, his smile spreading. I looked for my mother – might she help? Where was she? I could hear the TV on in the lounge, but I couldn't see her. 'He says *get in*,' she yelled from the sofa.

It looked dark in there, I could only see the outline of bags and boxes and hear the wild tweeting of the finches she kept caged amid the junk. I scrambled for the light pull, but Tony grabbed my wrist in mid-air. With his other hand, he unscrewed the lightbulb and threw it into the hall. Then he pushed me in and slammed the door shut, locking it from the outside.

It was so frightening and claustrophobic with all the coats and boxes piled against the low sloping roof. I couldn't see a thing. The birds were going mad at the sudden chaos, flapping around causing dirty grit to fly from the cage. I had no idea how long I was going to be in there for. Would it be like the bedroom where I might not get out for days? Would I have to go to the toilet on the floor and get punished again?

Feeling about in the dark, I realised there was no carpet – just floorboards. It was so uncomfortable, but I was scared to start moving around in case the noise annoyed them. Slowly, my eyes adjusted to the darkness and with a small shaft of sunlight shining underneath the door, I could get a sense of the space. There was a hoover in there, more old boxes of cassettes and some old cooking utensils. There was a small container holding sticks of honeyed birdseed, which I wondered, if I got desperate, would I dare to eat?

It was hot and stuffy, my own body heat contributing to the temperature after the panic and adrenalin of running home. My knee was still bleeding, and I was desperately trying not to let it drip onto anything in case I got into trouble for it. Then I thought – where's Luke? Where had he gone? What if he thought we were still playing the game and he was waiting for me to find him?

Other children went away with their families and played with friends in the summer holidays, yet here I was, locked in a cupboard wondering if a beating awaited me on release. Why was this happening to me? Was I such a bad boy? Why wasn't I loved?

I knew I wasn't getting out for a while, so as quietly as I could, I arranged some coats on the floor to make myself more comfortable and closed my eyes – praying I'd be released before I suffocated. Then hours later, without warning, the door was unlocked and opened a fraction. I froze. Was I meant to get out or stay in?

Did I need to say sorry? Was it my mother or Tony who'd opened it? Was it a trick?

I gently leaned forward and looked through the gap. The air

smelled fresher, but it was dark, my muscles ached from cramp, but my bloody knee and tears had dried. Slowly, I peered around the door, shoulders and torso still inside. I could hear the TV from the lounge and guessed my mother and Tony were in there, so I edged out, shut the cupboard door behind me and waited in the hallway.

During an advert break, I heard my mother getting up from the sofa. I stood to attention and waited for her to pass me.

'What do you say?'

'I'm sorry.'

During that summer break, the under-the-stairs punishments were regular. If I was out of sight, I was out of mind for them. It's sad to say, but I got used to it and sometimes convinced myself that it was even cosy. Anything was better than a beating from Tony or having to swallow chilli powder for my mother.

I often lost all sense of time in there, but slowly learned to gauge whether it was day or night by the sounds coming through the cupboard door. The drone of news signaled it might be lunchtime, A *Blankety Blank* theme tune and Les Dawson's voice meant it was Saturday evening. Music videos being slotted into the VHS player was usually the start of a party, so after ten o'clock at night.

This was another place where I let my imagination run wild. Kate Bush's 'Running Up That Hill' and Status Quo's 'Dreamin'' filled my ears as I tried to picture the videos that went with them. I'd take flight in my mind with Madonna when she sang 'Holiday', like her, trying to 'forget about the bad times.'

I didn't even question the fact that my mother kept finches caged in the cupboard. Why would I? I knew no different so assumed it was normal. Sometimes when she let me out, she'd release the birds in the house too. They'd dart around, landing on top of the curtains, going from one end of the room to the other, but they didn't fly well because they so rarely had chance to spread their wings. Then one day, they were gone and I daren't ask why.

I still wonder where my brother and sister were when I was stuck under the stairs all those times. Was Tony in Claire's bedroom, beginning the grooming process? Did my mother know?

5

•

Humiliation

LUKE DIDN'T get off lightly. His punishments were less frequent but no less humiliating.

After one of our mother's parties, she caught him messing about with an ashtray full of cigarette butts. He was just a curious kid, picking one up and pretending to smoke it like a grown up. She grabbed the overflowing ashtray, slammed it down on the kitchen table and told him to eat the contents while I watched. Luke was crying his eyes out, trying to put the filters in his mouth and chew them, vomiting, as she looked on enjoying the spectacle.

'That'll teach you to go poking about, won't it?'

I felt sick watching him. It was way worse than the frozen fishfingers I'd been forced to eat. Part of me wanted to help him, to get them finished so the punishment would end, but I knew if I tried, she'd find more and make me eat my own plate of them.

I was overwhelmingly thankful she hadn't seen me snooping in her bedroom the previous week when, amongst my stepdad's stash of porn, I found a bottle full of orange liquid. Thirsty, I took a quick swig but immediately spewed it out when I realised it wasn't Fanta. I suspected it was urine and felt sure she'd have made me drink the rest of it if she'd caught me.

It's no wonder Luke ran off as much as he did. If I'd been braver or known where to go, I would have too. There wasn't an ounce of love or comfort in that house. Even my mother's dog, kept outside in all weathers, was treated better than her sons.

Richie – Who Cares?

I was scared to death of that dog. It was a mixed breed with a wide mouth and lived in a dilapidated kennel on the end of a tether in our garden full of mess. She never cleaned up after it or took it for a walk. It wasn't socialised properly so growled when anyone came near. I avoided it at all costs, but my mother had obviously clocked my fear and added it to her weaponry.

Years later, with my life turned around, the irony was not lost on me that joy and success came from working with dogs – it was another two fingers to the past.

The time inevitably came when in her eyes, I'd done something wrong again. I'd asked for a shower after the boys were teasing me at school for smelling. That cold autumn evening, as the rain lashed down, I found myself being pushed out of the back door in my underpants, barefoot and told to stand in the garden near the growling dog.

'You want a shower? Well you can have one,' she said, laughing.

'But it's freezing. I didn't mean outside. Don't leave me out here, please,' I begged.

I was just inches away from the dog's snapping teeth as it pulled at the tether, feeling my fear. I'd been made to face the kitchen window, where the light inside illuminated her and my stepdad laughing and eating, doing their best to ignore me.

I had no meat on my body, looked like a rake, so I immediately started shivering. The humiliation was equally unbearable as mud and dog mess squelched between my toes as I hopped from foot to foot to try and keep warm. Knees shaking, fat droplets of rain dripped onto my shoulders and down my spine.

All the gardens on our row were overlooked by neighbours in the higher terraced houses opposite. Someone must have seen the state of me and tried to intervene by ringing the police or social services, because after what felt like an eternity, I was suddenly called inside and told to go upstairs to get clean and dry, quickly. Obviously, this was way before mobile phones were around, with easy-to-use cameras, so there was no evidence recorded – just one person's word against my mother's.

Crouched upstairs in my room, covered by just a towel, I heard people at the door. They sounded official and I could tell by the tone of my mother's voice that she was on the charm offensive.

'I tried to get him to come in, but you know what boys are like about playing outside. He's daft, that one,' she said.

Should I have run down and told them what had really happened? Would they have believed me? I knew it was pointless and I'd have ended up in even bigger trouble for telling, so I stayed silent in my bedroom.

'He doesn't do as he's told' said Tony, backing up my mother. 'We kept telling him he needed to come inside and get warm, but short of going out there and carrying him back in, there wasn't much we could do.'

Lies, lies, lies.

Throughout the whole of my childhood, people told lies about what they'd done to me to cover their tracks. I was learning that grown-ups said what they wanted to suit themselves - and they were largely believed. They either passed the blame or passed the buck, choosing the easiest route, regardless of the consequences for the child.

The official voices left the house, but I didn't move.

Why didn't those people insist on seeing me? They could have at least called out my name or made an excuse to use the toilet to get further inside – then they'd have witnessed how I was being forced to live. They either couldn't be bothered, or they fell for my mother's charm and chose to give her and Tony the benefit of the doubt. A major missed opportunity.

'Get dressed,' my stepdad yelled, 'then come down here and apologise to your mother.'

I put my smelly school clothes back on and did as I was told. 'I'm sorry.'

I think they might have been shaken by the authorities turning up at the door, because I was let off lightly and only sent to bed hungry. But I barely slept, I couldn't get warm.

I think my mother hated me more than Luke and Claire because she sensed I was gay, even from such a young age. In her mind, that made me a deviant, someone evil who needed curing. It's hard to believe, but my mother was religious. Or rather, she'd appear that way to others, but nobody with a Christian heart could have acted the way she did.

Every once in a while, my mother took me to the Sunday morning service at church behind my primary school. I never understood what the vicar was droning on about, it all seemed so dull. I hated singing from the hymn books because I still struggled with reading, but it was better than being stuck in my bedroom. At least she had her nice face on in church and I could pretend for a while that everything was normal.

But one Sunday, she humiliated me in front of the whole congregation. When the vicar asked if anyone needed special prayers, she took me to the front of the alter and told everyone that I was gay and wanted prayers to fix me. I couldn't believe what was happening. Everyone was staring and whispering, then bowing their heads to ask for forgiveness on my behalf.

I hadn't even had an experience with another boy. I'd only just turned eight. Maybe I'd said something to my mother about one of her previous boyfriends, or perhaps she saw me looking at men differently. I couldn't articulate what I felt and why. It is the way I am, but she saw it and didn't like it.

Afterwards, the vicar pulled me to one side.

'It's a sin. God doesn't love sinners,' he said.

'But I haven't done anything,' I said, bright red and indignant.

'God knows what's in your heart. He can see your soul. You need to ask for his forgiveness and guidance.'

I didn't understand. I hadn't done anything wrong. I thought that if God really could see into our hearts and souls, why wasn't he guiding my mother to be a better person? It didn't feel right that God thought she was good and I was bad.

The vicar put both his hands on my shoulders and looked into my eyes.

'He knows. He knows.'

What mother would do that to her own child? Especially in the late 1980s when the AIDS epidemic was still big news. And on top of that, section twenty-eight – the British law prohibiting the promotion of homosexuality by local authorities – had not long since been introduced by Margaret Thatcher.

That vicar was deluded. Surely, there must have been other church-goers with young children who could see how mortifying that incident had been for me. Considering we were in a so-called house of God, there was no kindness forthcoming.

After that humiliation, it was back home again.

'You're a deviant. I don't want a deviant in my family.'

'I'm sorry.'

6
•
Different Home

August 1991

I'D BEEN at Karen's house. Who knows what lies my mother must
have told to convince her to take me again after the head injury
incident. Maybe Karen felt sorry for me, but unbeknown to either
Karen or myself, we were both part of my mother's big plan that
day.

I'd been relatively happy, having played outside and been
allowed to eat lunch. But when it was time to go home, Karen said
that she was walking me back instead of my mother picking me up.
I was nine, so didn't question it.

When we got closer to our house, I could see there was a car
outside that I didn't recognise. It wasn't dad's Ford Capri, but
nobody else except him and grandad owned a vehicle in our family
– and grandad never came over. It was a red Vauxhall Nova in need
of a good wash, with furry dice hanging from the central mirror. On
the back parcel shelf, I could see a bunch of folders scattered across
the whole length of it.

Karen kept hold of my hand and continued to the back door
of our house. She knocked once and stepped in, gently nudging me
in front of her.

'He's back,' she called.

I could hear talking in the lounge, then it suddenly went
quiet.

'Be good,' she said to me, ruffling my hair.

Then she walked out and closed the door behind her.

I stood still, wondering if I was allowed to go into the lounge or not. The talking started again, and my mother had her nice voice on, so I thought it was probably safe to investigate. I slowly pushed the door open, standing half in, half out and waited for someone to say something.

There were five people in our tiny lounge. My mother, stepdad and a strange man on one sofa – and then Luke and Claire both squeezed into one chair together. Luke and Claire didn't look at me, but the grown-ups exchanged a glance between themselves. Nobody stood up.

The strange man had short dark hair and wore thick, square-shaped glasses perched on the end of his pale, greasy nose. His brown suit trousers and a white shirt looked out of place in our house. He was totally overdressed compared to the rest of us – he looked like a teacher.

He smiled at me, but it felt fake.

'Hello,' he said.

'Hello.'

'Go get some of your clothes and toys,' my mum interjected.

'Why?' I asked.

'Just get your stuff and bring it down here. We're going somewhere,' she said.

I had no idea what was going on. Were we going to Blackpool again? It was the summer holidays, so we might be. But Luke and Claire didn't look happy about it, if we were. I couldn't see *their* bags packed. But why would the teacher-looking man be coming with us? I hesitated, about to ask again, but thought better of it.

'It's alright,' the man said, 'nothing to worry about.'

But something in the way they were all sat there *did* make me worry. It didn't feel right. My mother was feigning upset, holding a tissue to her cheek and my stepdad had his arm around her. It was weird because I knew my stepdad wasn't kind and my mother never cried.

I made my way up the stairs to gather what few clothes I had.

Richie – Who Cares?

A couple of pairs of shorts and pants, a jumper and some socks. That was pretty much it. She said I had to bring toys too. What toys? I wondered. She'd locked them away. So, checking to make sure nobody had followed me, I quickly ducked into Claire's bedroom to take some of hers.

On the floor, right in the centre of Claire's room were my two cars – the police one with the missing wheel and the capri. Cruelly, she'd given them to my sister, hoping I'd see her play with them. I didn't have time to stand around though, so dashed over, swiped them up and stuffed them in between my clothes before heading back downstairs.

The man, my mother and stepdad were heading out of the lounge now. I could just see past them to Luke and Claire who were still sat on the chair together, staring at the floor, Claire wiping her eyes with the palm of her hand.

'This way,' my mother said, ushering me past the lounge door towards the kitchen.

'Where are we going?' I asked again – this time to the man.

'Don't worry,' she interjected.

'Yeah, don't worry' my stepdad said, waving and heading back into the lounge.

With my clothes and hidden toys clutched against my chest, I was gently guided in the direction of the car I'd seen on my way in. The man opened the driver's door, flipped his seat forward and asked me to clamber in the back as mum walked around to the front passenger seat. It felt stuffy in there – my legs hot against the grey and black fabric seats which had been warming in the sunshine.

Another big folder, identical to those on the parcel shelf, lay in the space next to me, papers spilling out onto the footwell amidst crisp wrappers and muddy shoe prints.

My mother buckled up and turned round to me, suggesting I do the same.

'We want to be safe now don't we?' she said.

I scrabbled round behind me, found the end of the seatbelt and clunked it into place.

As the man pulled away from our house, I had the feeling I

wasn't going back. Claire and Luke had come to the lounge window and were staring out at me, my stepdad behind them both, a hand on each of their shoulders, smiling.

We drove fifteen miles in silence. My mother kept her eyes forward all the way and the man made no attempt at small talk to comfort me. It was only when we pulled up outside a place called Willowdene that the silence was broken.

'We're here,' she said cheerily.

The man switched off the engine, stepped out and flipped his car seat forward again. I looked at my mother, but she refused to turn around.

'You'd better get out then,' she urged.

I was in front of a large, two-storey council building. There seemed to be loads of children in the drive, craning to see in the car.

'Ah, he's just a baby, he's so young,' I heard one of them say.

So young for what? I thought. I still hadn't been told what was happening, but by now I was beginning to wonder if it was somewhere to stay for a while. Maybe someone had told on my mother, and I wasn't going to be allowed to see her anymore. I turned around to look for her, but she stayed put in the car, seatbelt still on, as the man took my hand and my belongings, and led me towards a woman standing at the entrance to the children's home.

'Hello' she said, taking my hand from the mans'. 'My name's Jill. Shall we go inside and have a look around? Find your bedroom?'

My bedroom? So I *was* going to be staying here – but I had no comprehension as to how long for. The other children were swarming around me, closing in, trying to get a better look at the new boy. I just wanted to go back home to Luke and Claire. Why hadn't they come with me? What had I done wrong?

'What's happening?' I asked the man.

'Don't worry, everything will be alright. You'll be looked after here, won't he, Jill? We'll come back and see you soon.'

'Will my mum be coming back?'

'She will, don't worry.'

Jill's soft hand felt quite different to my mothers', and as I held it, I wondered if she was going to be kind or mean. Was this her nice face for the man and the other children? Would she be horrible once we were inside? Would she take me to the kitchen and make me eat chilli powder before locking me in a room? What if my bedroom was just like at home? My tummy was in knots as I tried to re-adjust to this new situation I'd neither predicted nor prepared for. I turned around just in time to see the car driving away with mother inside.

It was so noisy with the other children shouting and running around. I was the smallest one there, nine years old, scrawny, caught like a rabbit in headlights. Jill took me through the main door into a wide hallway with thick cream shiny paint on the walls, dirtied by wear and tear, peeling off in places. The floor was industrial type carpet – functional and definitely not homely.

To the right was an office, where I could see another man and woman, chatting and laughing. He was leaning back on two legs of a chair, arms behind his head while she regaled him with a story, using her hands to exaggerate strangling a child.

In front was a staircase leading to the residential social worker's bedroom. The children weren't allowed up there, but that didn't stop them, as I soon found out.

'This is the communal area,' said Jill, ushering me towards the room on the left opposite the office.

It felt huge, with long sofas, a TV area and a snooker table in the centre. The green baize was ripped in one corner and some of the pockets had been pulled off. The cues were discarded on the floor. Two boys stared at me as one whispered something to the other, causing them both to laugh.

Further down on the left was the dining and kitchen area, which was empty save for the cook, Christine, who was singing along to the radio. Christine was one of the nice ones. She was quite short – not much more than five feet on a cuddly frame, with shoulder length light brown hair. She looked to be in her early forties and wore double denim – jeans and a shirt. I could tell straight away she was kind.

When she saw me coming, she wiped her floury hands on her apron and turned the radio down.

'Excuse my singing,' she said, 'it's my favourite song, I always have to have this one on full blast.'

It was 'Seven Seconds' by Yousou N'Dour (ft Nenah Cherry). I loved that song too.

'You must be the newcomer then. Hello,' she smiled.

'Hello.'

'What sort of food do you like to eat? Are you hungry now? Do you want a biscuit?'

'Yes please,' I said.

She took the biscuit tin down from the shelf and opened it for me to choose one. She made everything from fresh, she said. I picked out a chocolate chip cookie and crammed it into my mouth as fast as I could. Delicious as it was, it barely touched my lips.

'There'll be plenty more where that came from, don't you worry,' she said, handing me another.

'Thank you,' I said, putting it in my pocket.

I followed Jill back out of the dining area, where the corridor split off left and right to the children's bedrooms. We went right, where some of the open doors afforded me quick glimpses inside. They looked better than my room at home, so that was one thing. I wondered if I'd be sharing with another boy since I shared with Luke at home.

'This is your room,' she said, unlocking it with a key from the outside.

'You can save up your pocket money and buy some posters to put up if you like.'

Pocket money? That was a first, I'd never got anything like that from my mother.

Jill told me what time tea was and reminded me where to go for it, then left me to settle in. She seemed nice. As soon as the door closed, I whoofed down the second biscuit then started looking at the room more closely. I immediately noticed it had a carpet, curtains, a light with a shade and proper bedding. There was just one bed, so I guessed this meant I wasn't sharing, which was a relief because I didn't know anyone. And the room was warm – that was lovely.

Richie – Who Cares?

The first couple of weeks at Willowdene were disorientating because I still didn't know why I was there. Nobody had told me. I tried to spend as much time as I could in my bedroom, away from the chaos, but it was weird being on my own, not sharing with Luke. I spent hours staring out of my window, trying to catch glimpses of activity in the ambulance station just behind the row of allotments. Whenever I heard sirens whir into action, I wondered what those medics were going to find, and thought how great it must be to have a job helping people and saving lives.

Where was I?

And why had I been left here?

Were the rest of my family still together at home?

I slept with the light on most nights – partly for novelty, but also because I was scared. I did manage to sleep during the first two weeks though, probably because I wasn't hungry and could use the toilet whenever I wanted. But something innate told me to keep myself to myself, to do as I was told, then I might be able to go home.

My mother made sure there was no chance of that when she arrived back at Willowdene a fortnight later. Even though I'd been secretly praying for her to come and get me, it was still a surprise when I walked through the door after school and found her stood in the hall with some of the other children.

I didn't know what to think. She had her nice face on, so I felt safe and wanted to run up to her and get my things and go back to Luke and Claire. Stupidly, a part of me wanted to show her my bedroom – that it was nice and warm and clean. I wanted her to know that I was alright, that I was brave. But mainly I thought, *finally, I'm going home.*

'Hi,' I said.

'Hello.'

It felt weird seeing her there, in the space where I'd been living for the last two weeks. I wasn't sure what to say to her or how to approach her. I didn't want to do the wrong thing and make her go away again. 'I'll just put my school bag away,' I said, heading towards my bedroom.

I walked past her and the children, feeling cautiously happy. I wanted the other kids to know I had a proper mum and was loved, because some of them had started bullying me a bit – nothing unbearable – yet, just name calling, shoving, showing me the pecking order. One of the older boys, Chris, had taken to mocking me whenever he got chance.

I slung my bag in my room and practically raced back to the entrance, where I just caught Chris asking my mother:

'Why's he at Willowdene?'

'Because he sexually abused his little sister,' she replied.

There were gasps all round. My mother smiled, triumphant.

She must have known what would happen to me in a children's home with a lie like that circulating.

'That's not true,' I shouted.

How could she? How could she say such a thing? And in front of all those other kids? It was a lie. I would never, ever touch or hurt my little sister in any way. I felt my face burning and my whole body shaking. This was so unfair. It was so monumentally untrue.

'That's a complete lie,' I repeated 'how could I have done? I don't like girls, you know I like boys,' I blurted. She had basically forced me to come out, aged nine, in front of the whole children's home. Suddenly, it felt like they all turned on me and began jeering, calling me names – batty boy, paedo, dirty freak. It was so frightening.

'Tell them it's not true about my sister,' I shouted.

Staff in the office heard the commotion and came running out, one of them grabbing my mother by the arm and briskly walking her away from the scene. As she was marched towards the car park, she twisted her face towards me so that I could see her smirking. 'He's a deviant,' she spat.

Jill was on shift that day, so rushed over and scooped me up, barging through all the kids to deposit me safely in the office. 'Wait there,' she said, walking back out and locking the door behind her.

I couldn't process what had just happened. Why had my mother come to Willowdene and told all the children that I'd sexually abused my sister? It made no sense at all and was cruel beyond belief. Not only did she want me to be unhappy in her house, but she couldn't bear for me to have a shred of joy elsewhere. I was crushed, the pit of my stomach shrinking in. Total rejection.

When my mother had been escorted off the premises, I put my ear to the office door and heard Jill and one of the social workers trying to calm down the rest of the children. It was pandemonium. My mother's words were carte blanche for them to do whatever they wanted to me from now on, and the following eighteen months saw me descend into a life which no child (or adult) should ever have to experience.

They kept me in that office for a long time, until everyone had dispersed. When Jill came back in, she sat next to me and held my hand, saying she was so sorry about what had happened, and asked if I needed a glass of water. Jill was then joined by another social worker, who got straight to the point.

'You need to be honest with us now. Did you in any way hurt your sister Claire?'

I couldn't believe he had to ask me – that he'd taken my mother's word for it.

'No,' I shouted in frustration, 'How could I do something like that? I like boys. I don't like girls. How could I? And she's my sister. I wouldn't do that. I didn't do that.'

'Okay, it's okay, we believe you,' said Jill.

But I got the impression the other social worker wasn't giving me the benefit of the doubt, seeming more bothered about me being gay, as if my sexuality went hand in hand with abusive behaviour. I could sense the revulsion at what he thought I was, what he believed I'd done.

Jill walked me to my bedroom, speeding up past the few kids who were hanging about in the communal area. I was the talk of Willowdene for all the wrong reasons. There was no way I was going to eat tea with everyone after that. I just wanted to hide away and cry, so when Jill closed the door, I crawled under my covers and sobbed.

Next thing I knew, there was a boy in my bed.

7

·

Criminalised

THE BOY was called Shane and he was sixteen. I'll never forget him. When something like that happens, you don't. I was woken up with the feeling of him pulling my pyjama bottoms down and laying behind me, something hard in my back. I froze.

He might have thought I was still sleeping, or he might not. But he certainly hadn't been invited in. It was confusing and frightening. He was breathing loudly in my ear as he tried to press his penis inside me. This was my first experience and I didn't know what was happening. I was thinking *is this what gay people do?*

I was lucky (if you can call it that) that he didn't actually get inside me. Instead, he put himself between the top of my legs and thrusted until he came. I laid there, not knowing what to do, keeping my eyes closed, pretending to be asleep. It didn't feel particularly violent. He didn't say a word or force me to do anything to him. He just did what he did and left.

After he'd gone, I daren't move for a long time. I was just left with his mess and my tears soaking into the sheets. I felt wretched. Why had he done that? Was it some form of punishment because he believed I'd abused my sister? Or was he gay and thought I'd be an easy target, having been forced to come out earlier that day?

I hardly slept, but the next morning I questioned whether it had really happened. The evidence was on the duvet though, so there was no denying what he'd done. I felt ashamed because I knew it wasn't right – but overriding that shame was fear. I didn't know what

Richie – Who Cares?

I was going to do when I saw him. He lived in the same building as me. His room was close to mine. I couldn't tell the staff because I felt certain he'd come back and do worse if I got him into trouble.

I tried to pretend it hadn't happened. If I didn't mention it, I reasoned, it might not be real, so I put my school uniform on and went downstairs.

Shane was sat in the communal area in front of the television. As I walked past, he turned his head away from the screen, stared at me blankly, then continued watching the programme. He never spoke to me, nor I to him. It only happened once with him, and shortly after, he was gone.

When I returned from school that day, everything in my bedroom had been moved upstairs to an area called The Crow's Nest. I'd been given another room, right next door to where the residential social workers slept. Did they know what had happened the night before? Or was I moved because of what my mother had said, and they feared for my safety? It just wasn't discussed.

Safeguarding wasn't a priority. There weren't even internal locks on our doors for privacy. Shane had been able to walk into my room while I was sleeping and do what he did. If staff thought that by simply moving me to another room, there'd be no more abuse, they were deluded. But what happened with Shane that night – compared with what was yet to come – was a walk in the park.

Everything changed from that day on.

They say 'sticks and stones may break my bones, but words will never harm me', but I couldn't disagree more. The children regularly started calling me puff, bender, bum bandit, batty boy, that kind of thing all the time, and it really got to me. I'd be beaten up just for walking past someone – punched, kicked, spat on, when all I wanted to do was blend in, be normal, get on with my life without fear and aggravation. My room was trashed so many times. They'd overturn my bed, steal my toys and throw rubbish into it. Sometimes the staff saw the mess and helped me put things back together, but the children who'd done it were rarely punished.

A boy called Kevin was the ringleader. He gradually dragged me down a path of crime, beginning with petty theft and ending with him pimping me out to paedophiles. He'd punch me for being gay, but then force me to perform oral sex on him. It was so messed up, the whole situation.

Every day was a fight for survival, and all the while I wondered where the rest of my family were and what they thought of me. Had my mother lied to Luke too and told him that I'd abused Claire? If so, surely Claire would have told Luke the truth. What about my real dad and my grandma and grandad? What had she said to them?

The first few times Kevin used me for his own benefit was for stealing. There was an off-license down the road from Willowdene – a basic corner shop selling the usual newspapers, milk, tins of beans, sweets and booze. There was generally just one person working behind the till, with only a poorly focused black and white CCTV camera. Kevin gave me orders for what he wanted then distracted the shopkeeper, while I'd pocket the goods and run.

I hated doing that. Even at a young age I had a real sense of right and wrong, but I had no choice. This bully lived in the same place as me. How could I have possibly refused someone so much bigger, knowing what he would do if I said no? He thought because I was only nine, that I wouldn't get prosecuted if I was caught. He never let me have anything that I'd stolen for him, not even one sweet.

He also used me as a look-out when he wanted to break into cars or steal bikes, making me stand at the end of the road to signal if anyone was coming. I always wondered what the person would think when they found their car afterwards. I hated that I was part of ruining someone's life, but there wasn't a shred of empathy from Kevin.

'They deserve it. They're rich,' he'd say. 'Why should they have stuff and not us?'

It didn't take long for Kevin's control to spill over into sexual acts. I'd become familiar to him – he knew I was mailable, corruptible, and after a few weeks he knew I'd do whatever he told me to do, because I was so frightened of him.

I was in my bedroom just messing about with my toy cars

when he opened the door and stared at me. It wasn't an aggressive look, it was like he was half-smiling. I shoved the cars under my bed and met his gaze. I thought he was going to tell me what he wanted me to steal from the shop, or say I had to go with him to be a look-out. But instead, he walked in and wedged the door closed behind him with a chair and, unzipping his trousers, he took his cock out and leaned back against the frame.

'Stick that in your mouth,' he said.

'What?'

'Come here, and stick that in your mouth, you puff.'

I looked around me, hoping to see a way out. There was no chance. He'd barred the door, and the window in the Crow's Nest was too high to jump out of without breaking an ankle. If I resisted, he'd beat me to a pulp.

I stood up and moved slowly towards him, praying that one of the social workers would knock on the door and save me. But I knew there was little chance of that, they'd be in their office, watching TV. As I got closer, Kevin grabbed my hair and pushed my face to his groin.

'Open your mouth and suck that,' he instructed.

It was awful. By now, I'd guessed that this is what gay men did to each other. But I didn't like Kevin. I hated him. The whole scenario was scary and awkward. I was still too small to kneel and reach that part of his body, so I half crouched as he forced my head back and forth, ramming himself into my mouth as I tried not to gag or bite him.

I willed it to be over and for him to leave me alone, but he continued with his fist grasped tightly around my hair until he came in my mouth then pushed me down onto the floor. I was gipping at the warm, slimy substance coating the back of my throat and tried to spit it out on my sleeve as fast as I could.

Kevin sneered as he watched me stand up and edge towards the window. Then he zipped himself back up, moved the chair from behind the door and swaggered out without a backwards glance. I stood there, numb. What had just happened?

It must have been a good half hour before I dared move, but

I was desperate to get to the bathroom where I could clean my teeth and get rid of the rancid taste of him. I never felt safe in that home because I had no idea when Kevin – or anyone else – might come looking for me.

The next morning it was a similar scene to what happened with Shane. Kevin pretended like nothing had happened, and wherever possible, I kept out of his sight and stuck near Jill or Christine. I couldn't stand to be near him, but he had other ideas. For him, that was just the start.

As late autumn turned to early winter, there were no warm, cosy evenings in with the staff and other children. While normal families enjoyed the mundane routines of preparing an evening meal, bath, homework and story at bedtime, Kevin opened my door and told me to get my pocket money.

'Follow me,' he said.

'Where are we going?' I asked

'Just get your money and I'll tell you when we get there.'

Obviously, I had no choice, and a small part of me felt relieved that at least he wasn't asking me to do anything sexual with him.

I got the few pounds I'd hidden under a Beano comic in my bedside table, grabbed my anorak from the chair and blindly followed him. Most staff were holed up in the office with the door shut, turning a blind eye. We were more trouble than we were worth – bad kids from bad homes doing bad things. No-hopers.

Hands stuffed into our pockets for warmth, we walked a short distance from Willowdene to the bus stop along the main road. I had to pay Kevin's fare too, then we made our way to the back of the bus in silence, watching the streetlights flashing past through steamy windows. Workers were on their way home, shops closing their shutters and inside the bus, commuters held bags over their tired knees, glad another day was done.

'Here,' said Kevin, after about fifteen minutes.

He got up and gestured for me to follow him.

I'd been *here* many times before. It was the Victoria Shopping Centre in Nottingham, but as everything was shutting, I knew we weren't about to start buying or stealing anything. Nearby was a block of concrete flats. They looked grim. The kind of buildings which blend into the general greyness of a precinct. I'd barely even noticed them before, but Kevin headed off in that direction, so I kept in step with him.

He opened the ground floor entrance door, and my first thought was that it stank of urine. It was cold, with graffiti on the dented, metal lift doors. I was beginning to feel scared. Where were we going? What was he going to do to me? Kevin pressed the lift button and when the doors opened, we stepped in over a bunch of discarded needles. He seemed to know exactly where we were heading, so pressed the floor number, waited for the doors to close then turned to me.

'Don't do anything stupid when we get there, alright?'

I nodded and waited for the lift to go up.

As the doors opened again, the corridor didn't look much better. We turned left and almost immediately, there was another door. Kevin knocked and waited, shooting me a warning glance as we stood in silence.

A tall, heroin-thin man with a pale, acne-scarred face peered around the cracked door. His mousy hair was cut short, revealing a dark thumb-sized tattoo just below one of his ears. His jeans were too big for his frame, his dark T-shirt stained with grease.

He stood back, motioning for us to go in. This felt all wrong. The flat was filthy; smoke hung over discarded tin foil wrappers on a battered leather sofa, and a low, grimy coffee table held beer cans full of ash. Behind the half drawn dusty curtains I saw the street below and guessed we must be on the fourth or fifth floor. I stood nervously, not knowing what to do or say as he eyed me up and down.

'Here's another one for you,' Kevin said to him.

The man in the flat circled around me, assessing what was before him. He was calm and when he finally spoke, I was shocked at the depth of his voice. 'Do whatever Kevin tells you, and everything will be fine,' he said to me.

I looked over at Kevin, who seemed very pleased with himself, like he'd passed a test with top marks. It was obvious they knew each other, but Kevin was his minion, he acted very differently around this guy. He wanted to impress him.

I was struck by Kevin's comment of 'another one' and wondered who else he'd brought here – where were they now? Panic was rising as I tried to focus on my surroundings, my eyes darting around the room looking for knives, guns, anything dangerous. Had I been brought here to be killed?

I daren't ask what he might want me to do. It wasn't the sort of place to ask questions, but as it happened, there was no chance to anyway. As soon as the guy finished speaking, he waved Kevin and I back out of the door. As it shut behind us, Kevin pushed me back towards the lift and pressed the button.

'You heard him. You do as I say.'

I nodded and got back into the lift with him. There was no point trying to run off, because I where would I go? Back to Willowdene, where Kevin lived as well?

He took me to Victoria bus station and set me to work as a prostitute. A rent boy. I was nine years old.

There were male toilets in the corner of the bus station, just near the steps by the road. It used to be a train station, so there was a huge hole in the ground where the platform once was. That's where I got my orders. Kevin told me to go into the toilets and try to catch a guy's eye. Anyone who was stood at the urinals, he said. If the person looked back at me, that was a sign that they wanted me to do something. He said they might nod or wink or just stare. I was told to ask if they were *looking for business*. It was horrendous.

'What do I do then, Kevin?' I asked.

'Do whatever they want you to do and charge twenty quid a time. Don't argue with them.'

There was no specific type of man, other than the fact they were all paedophiles. They were young, old, fat, thin, clean, smelly, single, married, rich, poor. As long as I did what they wanted me to do, and they paid me, it didn't matter to Kevin. I had to give him all the money I earned.

The first time, I was taken into a cubicle by a man and made to perform oral sex on him. I think that was one of the reasons why Kevin forced me to do it to him at Willowdene, so I was prepared. But more often than not, I'd be taken elsewhere and that was even scarier. The men would wait at the side of the bus station in their cars, near the taxi rank. I'd know, just by walking up to them, what they were after. Kevin sometimes spotted them before me.

'There's one. Go and see him,' he'd say. I'd have to walk over and repeat the same thing 'are you looking for business?'

Then I'd get in a car with a complete stranger and be driven off down a woodland track or near an abandoned building. There were regular places, where it was dark with nobody else around. It was absolutely petrifying. I honestly feared for my life, every time. And that was before I'd even done what they were paying for.

'If you tell anyone, I'll come for you,' was a regular threat. I was sworn to secrecy by the men who sexually abused me and the men who took my earnings.

At the beginning, it was mainly oral sex or hand jobs. I'd be in the passenger seat, and they'd be behind the wheel with their pants down. I really hated oral because sometimes they weren't clean. Sometimes it was so disgusting that I'd throw up in my jumper. They never wore a condom so it's a miracle I didn't catch HIV, but at the time, the prospect was the least of my worries.

I don't know how I got through that first night at the bus station. It felt like I was in a nightmare, watching what was happening to someone else. I went back into survival mode, trying to imagine I was in a different place like I did when my mother locked me in my bedroom or under the stairs. I can't remember exactly how many men I had to go with, but it felt like a lot, they all merged into one.

At some point though, I realised Kevin wasn't there anymore. Had he gone back to the flat to tell the pimp what I was doing? Or was he watching me from somewhere? It was so confusing.

I waited around for a while, not daring to leave but too frightened to stay. Eventually, I just got too cold and sick with nerves, and left. All I wanted to do was sleep and get warm. I still had enough money to catch a late bus home, so I took my chance to escape back to Willowdene. I paid my fare and shot to the back of the bus, hoping nobody could see me and felt like what I'd done was written all over my face. I wondered if the driver or other passengers could tell – and if they'd inform anyone. I slumped down in the seat, trying to make myself invisible. With one finger, I wiped condensation off the window to check I was heading in the right direction.

I was still on autopilot, holding myself together until I was back at the children's home and away from those men and the things they made to do. Every time the bus pulled up to a stop, I feared Kevin would get on and drag me back. It changed the way I looked at the other passengers and I felt there was no way of knowing if they were they type of people to use someone like me. In my head, everyone on that bus was a paedophile.

When we got to the stop nearest Willowdene, I waited until the very last minute before getting out of my seat, then made a bolt for the door. Once out, I ran all the way back without stopping, fearing Kevin could be lying in wait anywhere along the route. I knew better than to burst through the door and make an entrance, so I gently turned the handle and slid through. No staff were visible. All I could hear was a couple of the other kids in the communal area arguing over a game of snooker.

I crept into the kitchen, opened the fridge door and grabbed a handful of leftover sandwiches, stuffing one in my mouth and the others in my anorak pocket. I reached for the biscuit tin, hoping Christine had left something nice in there, but it was empty. Then I crept up the stairs to the Crow's Nest and let myself into my room, quietly closing the door behind me. With my back against it, I finished the stolen sandwiches and let the tears fall.

I still couldn't understand how I'd ended up there. If my mum didn't want me, why hadn't anyone else in my family come to my rescue? Was I really that bad? I knew I hadn't done what mum had told everyone, but why did she say it? Why did she make me have to say 'I'm gay' to prove I hadn't sexually abused my little sister? I felt so lonely and saw no end to what was happening.

I was trapped and feared worse to come.

8

•

Traumatised

KEVIN FORCING me into prostitution became a regular thing. He also ramped up his sexual contact with me inside Willowdene, so I never knew when he was going to turn up at my door and demand something.

Others continued with their name-calling, violence and room-trashing. I had nowhere to turn and repeatedly asked staff if I could call home, but my mother refused to speak to me.

In the run-up to Christmas, Kevin sent me out renting more often as paedophiles were keen to blow their seasonal bonuses on abuse. I never got used to the terror, but some nights were less frightening than others. There were two regular men who treated me a bit better – clean, relatively young, perhaps in their thirties, and sometimes brought me gifts. I still didn't want to be doing what I was doing with them, but I generally didn't throw up afterwards and they never tried to push more on me than we'd agreed.

I noticed a few men had families themselves, not that we discussed it, but I could see booster seats in the back of their cars or toys kicking about. Some wore wedding rings, as they cheated on their wives with a small boy.

I'd obviously been part of a wider ring of children being abused in Nottingham. I never saw the other minors though, but the way Kevin introduced me to the skinny man with the pock-marked face tells me now that I wasn't the first and wouldn't be the last child to have their innocence taken away so brutally.

Sad as it was, my first Christmas Day in a children's home was better than anything I'd experienced with my mother. There were presents for a start.

Willowdene had been all decked out by the staff and looked like Santa's grotto. The transformation was amazing with everything so colourful and bright. There was tinsel draped around the windows, red, green and gold foil stars dangling from the ceiling and an actual tree with baubles and fairy lights. I wished it looked like that all year around. A visitor to the home would assume Willowdene was a welcoming, happy place if they judged it on decorations alone, but everybody there knew the glitter was masking a grim reality.

The sparkling angels made it easier to pretend things might not be that bad though, and at least I got a reprieve from prostitution on Christmas Day.

That morning, I couldn't believe my luck when I got two whole bin bags full of presents.

'Are these really for me? Who are they from?' I asked, hoping some might be from my family.

'They're from all the staff here. And some are from the motorcyclists who donate presents every year.'

'Are there any from my mother?'

'Well, there are a lot in there, and not every parent can afford presents for their children.'

She hadn't bought me anything.

Not even written a card. But though that was bitterly disappointing, I was still desperate to rip open the gifts other people had donated. If they weren't from my mother, I didn't care who they were from. I just tore in, overwhelmed by the amount of clothes, colouring books, posters, crayons and felt tips. I got some new toy cars and buses, which I just loved and so many selection boxes. It was mind-blowing.

I looked around and saw everybody else had piles of presents too. Even the nasty kids. That didn't seem fair at all, but I didn't dwell on it because no sooner had I ripped everything open, I felt the need to hide my gifts in case they got stolen or broken.

Richie – Who Cares?

We had a full Christmas dinner too. Christine did turkey with all the trimmings – and pudding. There were crackers to pull, paper hats to wear and jokes. Amid all the excitement though, I kept thinking about Luke and Claire. What were they doing at home? Was my mother still locking Luke in the bedroom when I wasn't there? I hoped they'd got some presents too.

Unbeknown to Luke, he had only a matter of weeks left in the family home. In late January, he was taken to a children's home called Red Tiles, not far from Willowdene. More suspicious bruising had been found on Claire and the blame was placed on him. Either my stepdad convinced my mum that Luke had been abusing Claire, or my mum knew it was Tony, but most likely played along for fear of losing her husband.

I'll also never know why the authorities decided to keep Luke and I apart. If Luke had come to Willowdene there might have been half a chance that I wouldn't have been pimped out anymore. We might have been able to share a room, so I'd have felt safer. Kevin might not have been as brave if I had my big brother to protect me.

But that didn't happen. And the sexual abuse continued – both for me and for Claire.

The next time I saw Luke was at a supervised meeting in 1993. We had a few meet ups but they never ended well because for some reason he always took my mother's side. Luke told me that his transition into the care system was completely different to mine, that he was just taken to social services by my mother and left on the steps. I can't see how that would have actually happened, but that's what he said.

Once Christmas Day was over, there was hardly a moments' peace again. Willowdene was a hotbed of petty crime and serious sexual abuse. Nearby cars were always being damaged, and not just by Kevin. Any vehicles in the neighbourhood were at risk, as were the staff's. I could see some of it happening from my bedroom window in the Crow's Nest and always tried to keep an eye on Jill's blue Ford Sierra Estate, parked a little further back.

One of the older boys had been given a write-off car to tinker with after expressing interest in becoming a mechanic. It wasn't drivable, but it was obvious to anyone that he loved that rust bucket. He spent hours looking under the bonnet, checking the deflated tyre pressures or polishing the paintwork, taking great pride in having something to care for.

Then one night, it all kicked off. A riot at the children's home. I've no idea who or what started it but I hid away in my room and tried to barricade myself in. I heard children shouting and screaming, they were banging on tables and doors, hurling chairs and letting rip. Staff didn't stand a chance of calming things down so I crouched below my window, hoping the police or someone would arrive soon.

The riot moved outside and some of the older boys were jumping on top of the write-off car, hitting it with whatever they could find. Then they all worked together to lift it on its side and topple it over, windows smashing as it fell. I saw them pour something over it and set it alight, the whole thing whooshing up in flames, kids cheering and whooping. The boy whose car it was, nowhere to be seen.

I began to worry the fire would spread to the building and it burn down with me inside. Who would even know I was there? The staff weren't keeping tabs and I couldn't hear any fire engines on the way. I dared not leave my room but took some solace in the fact that while Kevin and the others were rioting, they weren't bullying or abusing me.

Eventually, the emergency services pulled up and the car fire was extinguished. Flames hadn't spread to the building, and nobody was seriously hurt. It was just one of many incidents where staff lost control and the children went wild.

Jill had an uncanny ability to sense when life at Willowdene was threatening to engulf me – and often stepped in. She'd find excuses to take me with her to buy supplies for the home, or sometimes, we'd drive back to her house singing along to UB40 tracks 'Red Red Wine' and 'Cherry Oh Baby'. Watching Disney films in her lounge, with her gorgeous golden Labrador on my lap, I would begin to feel calm again. For a while.

Whenever Kevin turned up at my bedroom door demanding

sexual favours, I knew the drill. I'd somehow de-sensitised myself to his attacks because they became so regular, that they were just part of my day. They were preferable to getting into a car with a stranger and being driven down a country lane, not knowing if I'd make it back in one piece. At least with Kevin, I knew he didn't want to kill me because I was worth more to him alive.

The final violent sexual assault on me inside Willowdene happened about eighteen months after my arrival – but it wasn't at the hands of Kevin. It was so bad that the staff had no option but to intervene this time.

Jake was a different kettle of fish.

He was roughly the same age as Kevin and often bullied me for being gay – verbally and physically. I was scared of him, but he never usually pursued me to the extent that Kevin did.

I just hadn't seen this coming.

'Hey, come here a minute' he shouted from behind his half-closed bedroom door.

I couldn't ignore him. He'd obviously spotted me and decided he was going to taunt me or beat me up. I hesitated, then moved towards the entrance to his door, but I couldn't see him.

'I'm here,' he said, stepping forward, completely naked.

My eyes widened and I immediately tried to run back out, but he'd been planning this. Before I had chance, he towered above me and slammed the door, jamming it shut. I looked to the window, but he'd locked it and drawn the curtains.

There was no escape.

What followed was so traumatic that I struggle to think about it. He went into a full-on, violent, sexual attack. He wasn't asking me to do things to him – he wanted to penetrate me and began tearing at my clothes, throwing me forward onto his bed. I screamed. 'No. Don't. I don't want it. Stop'

Someone heard my shouts of terror because as Jake continued his attack, hurling punches and grabbing me, staff started yelling for him to stop whilst trying to break the door down. But that just seemed to fuel his anger. I was begging him not to, pleading for him to stop. He got me into position.

Staff realised they couldn't get through the door, so ran outside around the back to try the window. With it being locked, they had no way of prizing it open, but could see through the chink in the curtains what Jake was doing to me. They smashed through the glass, but by then it was too late. He'd raped me.

I don't know how they got him out of there or what happened to me in the immediate aftermath. I assume the police were called and he was taken away. But over the next few days the atmosphere in Willowdene changed. It was like everyone knew that Jake had gone too far, and a sense of shame hung in the air.

My next memory is of leaving Willowdene. It was a cold, wet, February afternoon in 1993 and with no big explanation, I was told to pack my belongings because I was moving somewhere better – to another children's home, called Farmlands.

I was worried about going to a different place, even after everything I'd been through at Willowdene but, mainly, I was incredibly relieved because it meant no more Kevin, which meant no more prostitution, abuse or beatings.

It didn't take long for me to pack a couple of cases and as soon as they were zipped up, a social worker carried them to the boot of the waiting car. I held onto a toy bus in my anorak pocket, and as I followed her through the hall, Kevin sidled up beside me.

'If you tell anyone about me,' he whispered, 'I'll find you and kill you.'

I absolutely believed him.

I kept walking towards the vehicle and got into the back seat, trying to keep my eyes focused forwards. I strapped myself in and squeezed the toy bus in my pocket. As we were pulling away, I allowed myself a quick glance back, where I saw Kevin at the window of the communal room, pointing an angry finger at me, gesturing that I'd be dead if I said a word.

The car journey to Farmlands didn't take long, it was only about twenty minutes from where I used to live with my mother. On the way there, I vowed to myself to put what happened with Jake, Kevin – and everything else associated with Willowdene – as far out of my mind as possible.

We reached Farmlands down a long drive to a cul-de-sac. It was run, like Willowdene, by Nottinghamshire County Council. It looked like three terraced houses all lined together, with an L-shaped kitchen attached at the back. The whole building was very narrow, which made it highly conducive to conflict. It was difficult not to bump into people in the corridors, giving ample excuses for fights or unwanted sexual contact.

Nobody seemed to take ownership of the communal lounge area, so it was tatty and unwelcoming. For me, it was a place to avoid from day one. The only time I ever went in there was if I was summoned by the older boys or if one of the few nice social workers suggested a board game or activity.

But my bedroom was mint.

It was on the top floor at the end of the corridor, past the staff bedroom. It was the best because it had two windows – a big double one and a small single one, looking out onto the car park. When you walked into my room, there was a wardrobe on the left, the windows ahead, and my bed in the corner behind the wardrobe. I was happy my bed was there because I didn't want to sleep near the windows.

They were short-staffed, just like most council-run children's homes across the country. I encountered many adults in varying roles throughout my time in care, that it was hard to keep track of who did what job. A *field* social worker will have found a place for me at the home but wouldn't have worked there themselves. *Residential* social workers work in the home and are charged with looking after the group of children as a whole. They often stay overnight. Then each child has a *keyworker* assigned to them, which is meant to be more in-depth care, the go-to person for that child. My keyworker was Rose, who was lovely.

Altogether there was a manager, three assistant unit managers and about ten to twelve residential social workers, who all worked in shifts. They usually started at two o'clock in the afternoon with a handover from the staff on the previous shift. The staff who slept over brought their own bedding, which they stripped down after every shift ready for the next person. Their room was less homely than the children's bedrooms because no one person could put their stamp on it.

That's how things were *meant* to be run. But shifts were almost always extended, staff called in sick and the bulk of those on the payroll were doing it for money, not love. I never felt like I was in a nurturing environment and, at times, the place was completely feral. Out of all those adults at Farmlands, just three had my best interests at heart – Rose, Avril and Gary. If it hadn't been for them, I dread to think where I'd be now.

I was the new kid again, entering another lion's den. Farmlands felt harsher than Willowdene because in addition to staff spending a lot of time in the office, avoiding children, they also kept everything under lock and key, acting more like jailers than carers. Even the kitchen cupboards were bolted so there was no chance of growing teens grabbing a snack or drink between meals.

Despite everything, my first couple of months at Farmlands felt relatively calm. I wouldn't say I settled in or felt relaxed, but there was no sexual abuse, and as yet, the other children didn't know anything about my past. I mainly stuck with the staff, and even struck up a friendship with another boy, Tim.

Tim was a bit younger than me and was the only one who seemed to be on my wavelength. He was black and quite short and got picked on for the colour of his skin. I suspected he was gay too, but he wasn't the type of person to come out at the time. As far as I know, the abuse Tim received was racial, not sexual, but I had an affinity with him because like me, he was being bullied for *something*.

Tim's bedroom was opposite mine, we were the two right on the end, so we quite often talked and played Michael Jackson music because he was a massive fan – he basically wanted to be him. Tim was eccentric in his own way. Quirky. Funny. Just lovely.

Then one night when I was late back from school, Tim told me what had happened whilst I was out. A member of staff had gathered all the children into the communal lounge and announced that he had something to tell them. He wanted to warn them about my lifestyle.

'He is a rent boy,' he'd said.

So that was that. No more peace for me.

Just when I'd dared to hope that the enforced prostitution had come to an end at the hands of Kevin in Willowdene, someone worse stepped up to take his place in Farmlands – Brett. Kevin had been abusive and controlling, but Brett took it much, much further, eventually landing himself in jail and me in a secure unit.

Brett was stocky, broad, with lightish hair and crooked teeth. He had a manic look in his eyes and a misguided arrogance. His temper could switch in an instant and I'd have no choice but to do what he wanted me to. All the children in Farmlands were scared to death of him.

After hearing the announcement about me being a rent boy, Brett suddenly saw me as both a toy for himself and a money-making machine on the streets of Nottingham. He wanted me to penetrate him, and he wanted to penetrate me. I wasn't even eleven years old. He was mid-teens.

He had a sidekick called Carl who was about the same age as him and together, they basically ruled me. Carl was the physical opposite of Brett – tall, skinny, ginger and spotty. He usually wore tracksuit bottoms, T-shirts and trainers. From what I can recall, he also had mild learning disabilities.

Brett and Carl were sexually active with each other, but sometimes they tried to drag me in too. I absolutely hated every minute of it. They repulsed me.

I dreaded being penetrated by them. As a gay man, you are either what's called a top or a bottom. A top is someone who prefers to do the penetrating. A bottom is the one on the receiving end. It's obviously fine if you like both, as long as both parties are happy with the situation. But I am a top, so when another man is forcing himself upon me, it's rape.

Brett was completely unstable, with his temper extending to inanimate objects too. He once put his foot through a glass fire door – the sort with wire inside – because he was so angry about something. Nobody felt safe around him, staff included. He always seemed to know where I was and if he was in the mood to beat me up, he'd find me and pummel me until I was black and blue.

Unfortunately, whenever I wanted to go to my bedroom, I had to walk past Brett's.

Although Carl was sexually violent towards me when he was with Brett, his solo abuses were more controlled. Sometimes, he'd drag me into his bedroom and force me sit on his bed while he undressed, or he'd lurk in the toilets and trap me in a cubicle. It got to the point where I was begging members of staff to accompany me to the bathroom so I could go without being hassled. When they refused, I went to the girls' toilets instead, because their cubicles had locks on the doors.

Brett stayed at Farmlands for longer than he was meant to – until after his sixteenth birthday. I can only assume it's because they felt he was too much of a risk to be given that final bit of freedom.

As it happened, freedom wasn't on the cards for him anyway, for a very long time.

9

•

Abducted

I SUSPECT THAT Kevin and Brett were working for the same boss of the paedohpile ring I met in Victoria flats, but the only thing that changed was who I gave my money to and the location of abuse, Brett widened the scope to include some city centre bases too.

In addition to general prostitution within a few miles, Brett had me disappearing with men across the country for days on end. This felt like kidnapping, even though I had to *agree* to what I was doing. I was abducted three times in total, each incident so traumatic that, just like the one with Jake at Willowdene, I tried to block the memory out.

I hadn't been warned about any of these so I've no idea if they'd been set up prior or it was just circumstance, but the first one began in Nottingham city centre. A man in a white Vauxhall Combo van was driving slowly near a known place for punters. Brett was hovering around the corner out of sight but when he saw the van, he walked over to me.

'That one's a bit keen. He keeps looking at you and giving you the signal. Go and speak to him.'

My casual stroll over belied the fear in the pit of my stomach. I could never shed the dread of wondering if each new man might be the one to murder me. There was a real risk with every scenario.

He rolled down the window and smiled, trying to look friendly, and asked me to get in the passenger seat. He said he'd like to take me somewhere to treat me, so I got in and put my seatbelt on, then he drove round the corner, down a side street and stopped. 'How much is it for an hour?' he asked.

'It's sixty quid.'

'What if it's much longer than that?'

'Then it'll cost much more,' I said, sounding a lot more confident than I was.

The man came across as amiable, agreeable, not a nasty, violent monster. But I was only a kid, so he won't have wanted me to bolt before he'd got his way. We agreed a price and I assumed he was going to spend a few hours abusing me in an abandoned building or down a country lane.

'You're going to have to get in the back because I don't want you seen in front of the van,' he said, unclipping his seatbelt and gesturing for me to do the same.

This was new. I didn't like the idea of being bundled into a van at all. Was he going to get in as well and abuse me there?

He opened the back doors, and I could see it was completely enclosed. No window through to the front or sides. Strangely, it smelled sweet, like sugar. I looked at him and he motioned for me to clamber in, suggesting I sit in the corner, where I could lean against two sides. I did as I was told. The doors slammed shut and I could hear the lock turning. It was pitch black in there and I had no idea where I was going. The fear was making me need the toilet.

I began pleading in my head that I wasn't going to be driven to my death, wondering how on earth my life had led to me to this point. Did my mother know what I was going through? Would she care? Did Brett even know where I was going?

If I died, who would be bothered, and would I be found?

The journey seemed to take hours. The furthest I'd travelled from Nottingham before was Blackpool. In the darkness, I sensed we were driving on a long straight road, quite fast, and I wondered if we were on a motorway.

To allay the terror, I took myself back to the Madonna videos and imagined I was the priest in 'Like A Prayer'. I'd recently got into *Star Trek*, so hummed the theme tune and wondered what Captain Kirk would do if he was backed into a corner like this. I envisaged myself on The Enterprise. Except I wasn't on a mission to save the universe. I was in the back of a paedophile's van on my way to a weekend of sexual abuse.

Eventually, the van stopped. I sat dead still and listened for clues as to my whereabouts, but nothing sounded familiar other than the faint hum of traffic. I heard him get out of the driver's seat, his feet crunching on gravel as he walked around to the back of the van. The key clicked into the lock then he opened the doors wide, letting cool air and light flood in. I put my forearm across my eyes to shield them.

'You can get out here and come and sit in the front,' he said.

I shuffled forward to swing my legs out and looked around me. We were in some kind of wasteland, like an empty car park.

'Can I have a pee?' I dared to ask.

He checked nobody was near.

'Be quick. Just go behind the van,' he said.

As I relieved myself, I tried to get my bearings. It was scrubland with no discerning landmarks. We weren't far from a main road as I could still hear cars in the distance, but I couldn't see any signposts, and no buildings were close enough for me to tell what they were.

'Hurry up,' he urged, 'get in the front, next to me.'

I zipped up and got in the van. I daren't ask what he wanted me to do, so waited for instructions. But he put his seatbelt on, told me to do the same and we set off again. He said we'd be alright now because we were past the motorway cameras, and nobody would be suspicious with the two of us travelling together like this on the normal roads.

It was strange because he was very polite. We kept driving for about another half hour and I kept my eyes wide open, trying to pick up clues as to where we were going. I didn't recognise any of the names of towns or villages on the signs, but as the roads got busier, I spotted an open-topped red double decker bus emblazoned with pictures of London Bridge and Buckingham Palace.

We're in London, I thought. Somewhere in London.

Eventually, we pulled up behind a row of run-down shops

and restaurants, where he primed me to say I was his nephew, if anyone asked.

'How long will I be here for?'

'I'll probably take you back on Sunday,' he said.

He unlocked a dirty-looking door and I followed him up some much cleaner narrow steps until we reached the top with a door either side. He opened the red one on the right.

'After you,' he said.

The first thing I noticed were piles of fancy chocolate boxes everywhere – and that same sweet smell from the back of his van. He smiled when he saw me looking.

'I'm a chocolatier,' he said, 'help yourself to any you want.'

He told me more about his job and it sounded like he was a rep for a high-end chocolate maker. His flat was modern and immaculate with a few arty prints on the walls, but no pictures of family or friends. He seemed relaxed, acting like this was all completely natural, like we were just two pals or lovers chilling at home.

As he busied about in the kitchen, I got a better look at him. I guessed he was in his late forties, dressed in smartish jeans and a shirt tucked in over a small paunch. His hair was receding, but it wasn't greasy and when he slipped his shoes off, I noticed his socks looked expensive. He was at least a foot and a half taller than me, and his hands didn't look like they'd done much manual work. He looked soft and slightly pudgy.

He cooked for me, and we ordered whatever takeaway food I wanted, which he obviously paid for. I had to do my duty, carry out the role of someone being spoiled, being his boyfriend. It was the only way through because I didn't want to find out what might happen if I refused. I'd seen Brett switch to violence in a breath and feared this man might do the same. I never knew what punters were capable of and didn't want to end up dead.

We stayed in the flat for the whole weekend.

In amongst the boyfriend role-playing, there was also a lot of sexual activity. He would perform oral sex on me, and I'd have to do it to him. There was a lot of body contact.

He kept asking if I was ok with what he was doing. 'Yes, that's ok,' I lied.

He must have felt less guilty about abusing me if he heard me say I didn't mind. I just had to put my thoughts elsewhere and get it over with. Let him use my body and get the money so I could give it to Brett and not get beaten up.

He acted like he cared too, washing my clothes and letting me take my time in the bath or shower. He gave me various gifts including a remote-controlled car. But when we went to bed at night, and he had fallen asleep, spent, I lay there listening to the traffic and his snoring, trying to form an escape plan.

I knew where the door was, but not the key. I knew where the window was, but it was too high to jump. He hadn't given me any money by this point, so I'd have to find his wallet. If I got caught, what would happen? If I escaped, where would I go? I tried to close my eyes and think of anything else, but all I that came to me was how much I missed my brother and sister – and even my mother.

When daylight came, he continued his cycle of abuse before getting up, then showered and made me breakfast. He told me to get clean and dressed because he was taking me back. It was odd. I didn't feel safe, but it didn't feel as dangerous as other situations I'd encountered. He'd tried to normalise the situation.

The return journey was the same. I sat in the front seat while he drove for about half an hour back to the scrubland area, then I moved into the back of the van to be driven to Nottingham. Or at least, I hoped that was where I was going.

I was exhausted after a weekend of letting this man pleasure himself with me however he wanted. Even when he wasn't physically abusing me and we were watching TV, I was still on high alert. I must have fallen asleep because the next thing I knew, the door was being opened down a quiet road on the outskirts of Nottingham and I was told to get out.

'Don't forget your stuff,' he said.

My *stuff* was a plastic carrier bag holding the remote-controlled car, a load of England football merchandise and the cash for Brett. I had to walk the rest of the way back to Victoria station, then get a bus back to Farmlands. It was a small relief to be back on familiar soil, but I wondered if Brett would be in or if the staff had even noticed I'd gone. What would I say if they had rung the police? Would I dare tell? This time, I thought I might do.

I tried to keep a low-profile walking through the entrance to Farmlands, but I was spotted. There were no nice staff on that day, I was called into the office and shouted at for not telling them where I'd been. No caring words of concern. They took the plastic carrier bag off me 'for safe keeping' and told me to go to bed.

As I walked away, I heard them rustling through the contents and knew I was never going to see the car, football stuff or money again. Brett was going to kill me.

He was waiting by his door. He'd heard me come in and demanded his money.

'It's in the carrier bag that the staff just took off me. They wouldn't let me keep it,' I pleaded.

He beat me up, badly, and if the staff heard, they didn't intervene. I had spent a frightening weekend being sexually abused by a man I didn't know in a place I'd never been to, only to return to the children's home for a violent beating.

When I finally crawled into bed, I cried myself to sleep, too exhausted to think of a way out of this nightmare. I wasn't safe here or out on the streets. I was bullied at school and nobody in my family cared. I was sinking.

10

•

Pauline and Anna

THEN SOME respite came in the form of one of the loveliest women I have ever met, a link worker called Pauline. It was Pauline's job to take me out of the home once a week for about an hour, for a different perspective, doing anything from going to the cinema, park or shops.

We were introduced in the office at Farmlands and as soon as I saw her smiley Afro-Caribbean face, I immediately liked her. She says I looked like a scared little baby at the time, but we just clicked, and it wasn't long before our sixty-minute meetings once a week were extended to four or five hours, twice a week.

'Do you want to show me your room? Tell me what kind of games and things you like?' she suggested.

For once, I didn't feel like I had to run the gauntlet to my bedroom. With Pauline by my side, I could pass Brett's room without fear because friendly as Pauline was, I instinctively knew she was not someone to be messed with.

I showed her my *Star Trek* posters and told her how much I liked watching the TV series, because the good characters always did the right thing. In fact, it sounds strange, but I became a bit obsessed with the programme. Watching it was a complete escape. It made me feel safe and I'm still a huge fan to this day.

I showed her my boxes of cars and buses and said that what I *really* wanted in my bedroom was a goldfish, but that I wasn't allowed to have one.

That very day, Pauline spoke to the staff about my wish for a goldfish and with a bit of persuasion they relented. Together, we went to the pet shop in town. I was so excited to be getting my own fish – with a little bowl and some ornaments in it too. I was like a jack-in-a-box in that shop, bouncing from tank to tank, not knowing which one to choose.

'I like that one.... no, that one....'

I got two in the end. Pauline let me sit in the front seat of her car on the way back, where I balanced the clear knotted bag of water, holding the fish, on my knee.

'Drive carefully Pauline, I don't want to hurt them,' I said, nervous of them spilling out.

In my bedroom, we created a space for the bowl on the table next to my bed. After putting some special gravel in the bottom and placing the ornamental bridge right in the middle, we poured in some fresh water halfway up, and slowly dipped the bag with the fish in to get them used to the different temperature. Carefully, like the lady in the pet shop said, I tipped the bag and released the fish into the bowl and watched them swim around in their new home.

'They look like they'll be happy there,' said Pauline, standing back to admire them.

'I hope so. I'm going to look after them really well and keep them safe.'

'I know you will. When I see you next week, you can tell me how they're getting on and if they're enjoying their fish food.'

I didn't want Pauline to go and wished she could take me and the goldfish home with her. I knew as soon as she left, things would be bad again.

'Can't you stay a bit longer? We could watch them swimming,' I said.

'I tell you what, maybe next week you can come to my house for tea, would you like that?'

I said I would, and she agreed to collect me at the same time. I couldn't wait.

Pauline's house felt like a proper home. It was warm and cosy and smelled of the lovely chicken, rice and sweetcorn she regularly cooked. I played with her own children, then sat down at the table with everyone to eat. It was like being wrapped in a blanket of love and I never wanted to leave. Whenever it was time to go back, I always asked to stay a bit longer.

'I'm not ready yet Pauline.'

'Come on now, we can do this again. You know you've got to go back.'

My tummy started doing flips because I knew what was waiting for me at Farmlands. But Pauline came in with me and usually waited until I'd had a shower and put my pyjamas on. Then she'd tuck me in, and we'd talk about what we might do the next time. If I was very lucky, I wouldn't be bothered by Brett that night and I could fall asleep looking at my fish.

It wasn't long until my birthday – July – and Pauline wanted to arrange a party for me at Farmlands and invite my mother.

'She won't come Pauline. I know she won't'.

'Of course she'll come. I spoke to her on the phone twice to confirm and she says she'll definitely be here.'

While I was at school that afternoon, Pauline asked some of the staff at Farmlands to help her decorate the communal lounge with balloons and streamers. They brought in one of the tables from the kitchen and spread it with party food – mini sausages on sticks, crisps, sandwiches and even a birthday cake.

When I walked in, I thought it looked fantastic. A few of the other children were there with a handful of staff and they sang happy birthday as I blew out my candles. It felt special opening presents with Pauline there.

My mother didn't come.

We waited, but I knew she wouldn't. That's how she was. All nice and friendly with other people, promising this that and the other, but she saw her absence at my party as another chance to hurt me. She didn't even send a card. Ever. Not one birthday or Christmas card in all the time she lived.

In a photograph of that birthday party, Pauline looks furious. Brett had been in the room when it was taken, and he was trying to spoil everything by throwing racist comments at her. After the party, when Pauline left and everything was cleared away, I got my present from Brett. It wasn't nice.

Over the next few weeks, I completely lost my appetite and felt utterly trapped. If I didn't work for Brett, then I'd get beaten up or worse. If I *did* work for Brett, there was still a high chance of a beating anyway. I was damned if I did and damned if I didn't, doing things I hated, with men I hated even more. Eventually, I plucked up the courage to tell a member of staff about what happened in London.

I told her about the chocolatier, making it clear that I was doing it under the instruction of Brett and that I didn't have any option of disobeying him because he was so violent. I laid out the consequences of me refusing to do as he said. I thought that if the paedophile was caught, it might scare Brett and he might back off.

She listened to everything I said then rang the police. They suggested she brought me to the station so they could take a statement.

Once there, we were both led into a small but comfortable room by a policewoman and when we were settled, I was encouraged to tell them everything. I gave a description of the man, said where he'd picked me up and what he'd done to me.

Because I'd been moved to the front of the van once we were off the motorway, I could remember some of the place names from the road signs we passed. I've got a weird photographic memory for things like that. The police took what I was saying seriously, because they arranged for me to be driven to London, to the first road sign I'd seen, then from there, I was eventually able to direct them to the row of shops above which was the man's flat. Further down the line I was also asked to give evidence via video-link and felt hopeful all this all might come to an end.

I was never told the outcome of that investigation but I believe he was eventually caught. It didn't stop the abuse, as I'd hoped. I was kidnapped a further twice, once was to Leicester and the other was closer to home. Again, I told staff at Farmlands and in turn, they informed the police. I was interviewed again and managed to direct them to where the abuse had occurred.

Richie – Who Cares?

Unfortunately, word got back to Brett that I'd grassed and because I was so petrified of him, I ran away, missing important court dates which could have led to further convictions and the cases were dropped due to me being unavailable to give my evidence.

What I still really struggle to understand is why on earth this wasn't pursued. Why was nobody looking into the fact that a frightened little boy had run away because he was so fearful of the consequences in his own home setting?

That was one of the main parts of the problem – I had absolutely no escape. If the staff at Farmlands knew that Brett was the one forcing me down that line of abuse, then why wasn't he removed?

Time and time again, my desperate cries for help and obvious need for adult interventions were ignored or explained away. I was just a kid in a care home, adrift in a system with homophobic staff whose main priority was an easy life.

The care I received as a child was wholly dependent on the attitude of other adults, and though many were lacklustre at best, some, like Rose, Avril, Gary and Pauline, were nothing short of guardian angels. Another of those angels was Anna Daiches, who took action after reading a newspaper article about exploited children on the streets of Nottingham, in which I featured.

The journalist had taken me and another boy to McDonald's and asked us loads of questions while we were eating. I suspect the other boy was Brett, because I remember thinking I had to say what I was doing with all these men was my own choice, and that I wanted to do it for money, to buy toys and sweets.

But what journalist takes a child's words at face value and prints them? Had he tried to corroborate what I'd said with staff at Farmlands? Even bothered to find out why I was in care in the first place? Or looked into where this paedophile ring was based? The only saving grace was that he changed my name and blurred the photographs. It was nothing short of headline grabbing at the expense of vulnerable children.

That article did bring Anna into my life though, which was a blessing in so many ways.

She was studying for a Masters' degree in child clinical psychology at Nottingham University, and part of her course involved clinical practice in something called play therapy. After reading the report, Anna was annoyed at the sensationalism of it and felt there was too much emphasis placed on the sexual side of things and not enough on the root causes of behaviour. She got in touch with the editor and told them as much. Then she made enquiries into the possibility of helping me, as part of her degree. Farmlands were more than happy to oblige because her time was free and it meant I'd be out of the home on a regular basis.

Play therapists use play to help children process issues that have been pertinent in their lives. It's not directed, so they don't tell the child what to do, they go along with whatever the child's doing, to create a relaxed, safe setting, where their feelings can hopefully come to the surface. My sessions were based at the university, in a big room with a one-way mirror for experts or students to watch from the other side. The sessions were often recorded for further examination or for use as proof towards exam grades.

I loved that room. It was full of toys and things to do. I played in the big sand pit for hours, building and destroying things. The dressing up rack meant I could pretend to be different people – sometimes I was a parent abandoning then rescuing a child, or shouting at them, telling them to get in their room. Or I'd make one of the dolls eat something they didn't like.

I saw Anna once a week for at least a year and really enjoyed our time together. It was an exciting place to be, and she was always very kind. I was about twelve years old by this point and we quickly formed a bond. The play therapy sessions were good for both of us, because Anna was getting her case study and I was receiving much needed psychological help. But nobody expected her to go above and beyond to quite the level she did.

At some time during these sessions with Anna, my stepdad was successfully convicted of sexually abusing my sister and jailed for three years. To me, this proved mine and Luke's innocence beyond a shadow of a doubt. But by now both my siblings were in different care settings and I still had no contact with my mother, so there was no discussion about it. It was like nobody wanted to hear the truth and I couldn't understand why.

Pauline was in the picture though, so I asked her to take me to see my real dad who, by coincidence, lived on the same estate as her.

'I'll have a word with him and see if it's okay for you to come,' Pauline promised. Surprisingly, my dad agreed and the following week, holding my hand, Pauline took me round there.

I felt nervous about seeing him again. The last time we were together, I can't have been more than three or four. I wondered if he would look any different, if he'd be pleased to see me or had heard about my stepdad's conviction. If he had, then he'd know for certain that it wasn't me or Luke who'd abused Claire.

My dad hadn't been part of my life since the day he left when I was four, but he was never nasty to me. I can't remember him hitting me or taking part in any of mum's barbaric punishments, but he was far from the type of guy I wanted to grow up to be. He was weird – a pest controller with a passion for knives.

Pauline knocked on his door and after a while, I heard footsteps approaching from inside. He opened it lazily, like he was expecting to see some guy flogging him cleaning products rather than his son whom he hadn't clapped eyes on for years. I could see it looked grim inside, but we never set foot in the place.

He came out and closed the door behind him.

'Hello dad,' I said, smiling.

'Hello,' he nodded.

We stood in his front yard for less than half an hour and as a young boy, I got the distinct impression that he didn't really want me there. No hugs were offered, no conversations about how I was feeling, what it was like at Farmlands. None of that. It was all about his new wife, their children and his step-children. It was like I was some distant relative from another time with no relevance to his current situation.

'You know what happened with your sister. I shouldn't really be seeing you,' he said. So my dad still believed I'd abused Claire, even though Tony was in jail for it. My mother had somehow managed to drip her poison into his ear to make him think that as a seven-year-old boy, I had done that to a sister I loved.

'But I didn't do it dad. It wasn't me. It was Tony and now he's in prison.' He just kind of brushed over it and shifted on his feet. It wasn't something he wanted to talk about, and I was too scared to push it in case he made me leave. He was my dad after all, so any small nugget of time with him was better than nothing, however awkward.

My dad could have faced the truth, taken me out of that children's home and brought me up at his house, with my siblings. I don't know why he didn't do that. Did he think I was a danger to his latest children with his new wife? I suspect he knew that I didn't hurt Claire, but it was easier for him to go along with the lie to avoid taking responsibility for me.

Pauline did her best to keep the conversation going between us all, telling him a bit about Farmlands and how I often went to her house for tea. I told him that the boys weren't very nice to me and wished I didn't have to stay there, but he wasn't interested in any of it and eventually, made his excuses.

'Right, well, I'd better be getting on,' he said.

What was he getting on with?

Pauline thanked him, and I could tell she was hoping dad would lean forward and at least touch my arm, even if he couldn't bring himself to hug me. But no. There was no fatherly touch.

'We might come again then?' I asked.

'Maybe,' he said, closing the door.

I looked up at Pauline, feeling completely lost. It wasn't the visit I'd been hoping for. There was just no love there at all. She tried to hold my hand as we walked away, but I felt too cross about everything and batted her away. But as we headed back to Pauline's house, I revealed what it was like living with my mum after dad had gone, telling her about going to bed hungry and stealing food from the freezer with Luke – and not being allowed any toys.

When we arrived at Pauline's, we sat in the lounge on the sofa together and watched TV. She put her arm around me, and I snuggled in. We didn't say much, but after a while, she gently got up and straightened herself.

'How about chicken, rice and sweetcorn for tea?'

I smiled and nodded. She knew exactly what I needed.

I could hear her in the kitchen clattering pans around, boiling rice up, getting things ready. The space where she'd been sat next to me on the sofa grew cold, but I was warm inside, anticipating a delicious tea, made with love, surrounded by her family. She kept bobbing her head around the door to check if I was alright and when the food was finally cooked, she called everyone in. I couldn't eat fast enough, filling my belly right to the brim. When I finished, I caught her looking at me all thoughtful.

'Because you like this tea so much, I'm going to show you how to make it yourself. Then when you're grown, you can cook it too. Would you like that?'

I said I would.

Too soon it was time for me to go back to Farmlands again, and this time more than any other, I was desperate not to leave. It seemed so unfair that I wasn't part of a family like this. I didn't want to have to dodge past Brett's bedroom, then lay in bed, wondering if he was going to let himself in and abuse me.

'I'm not ready to go yet,' I said.

'I know you're not sweetheart, but we've to take you back.'

'But they're not nice to me there. They bully me and call me names. They call me rent boy and nasty names.'

'Well, you be sure to tell the staff about them. They've no right being mean to you. They don't even know what they're saying.'

The staff didn't listen. What was a bit of name-calling to them? I wasn't worth the paperwork that accusation would create. But, as ever, Pauline took me up to my bedroom and waited until I was settled. She tried to take my mind off things by asking how I was doing with my spellings at school and tested me with some of them.

'Next time we'll make that lovely chicken together. You dream about that now,' she said, kissing the top of my head and gently closing the door behind her.

11

•

Absconding

I NEVER ABSCONDED when Gary, Rose or Avril were on duty, but when they weren't around, life was extremely hard. The constant looking over my shoulder for Brett and Carl, the name-calling from the other kids, and when words didn't appear to be hurting enough, the violence.

That came from children in the surrounding neighbourhood too. Kids from families in normal homes beat me up because I was gay and I lived in a care home. They weren't even meant to be on Farmlands' premises but staff didn't stop them. And once anarchy was in mind, neither me nor the staff had a hope of stopping it.

I was in the back garden of Farmlands when a bunch of those children began throwing stones at me. Some of them didn't even know me but joined in, lobbing pebbles, watching them ricochet off the walls, one or two hitting the windows. It rapidly escalated into mayhem. I felt helpless as they laughed and jeered but then suddenly, I felt a real surge of anger rising. How dare they do this to me? Who did they think they were?

I picked up one of the slightly bigger stones and chucked it at one of the boys when he was retreating. I could have been a baseball player because I caught the side of his face and cut his eye. He let out a yelp and went running back to his parents, saying I'd started it all.

I was arrested for assault for that. Charged and cautioned by the police. No consideration given for the fact that I'd been goaded, or that the boys weren't even meant to be on Farmlands' property. No reprimand for the staff who should have been watching and intervening. That's just how it was. Care home kids were scapegoats, as I found out again on a more serious level a couple of years later.

But that was just another incident keeping me in survival mode. It was fight or flight and I was fast running out of strength. My absconding increased dramatically.

It was easy to slip out with staff always claiming to be in meetings in the office. But even when they were paying attention, I simply caught the bus to school, but didn't actually go. The first record of me running away was on 6th March 1993. I was ten. It says I came back the day after, having earned a fiver from a punter. On 9th March I told staff that I'd rather be back at Willowdene because I kept getting beaten up. On 10th March, two women found me in Nottingham city centre, brought me back and told staff I was being forced into prostitution.

Vague notes were taken, along with a promise of looking into the situation, but there was no follow up. The only thing the staff Farmlands did to protect me – a whole month after this pattern of absconding began – was to take my shoes so I couldn't run away. That didn't stop me. Sometimes I escaped barefoot in pyjamas, it was that bad.

Once I'd managed to get away from Farmlands, familiarity felt like my safest option, so I usually headed to a place near Victoria station. It was out of the way enough for people not to notice I was there, just down the side of the embankment. I hunted around for carboard boxes and made it my temporary home on more occasions than I can remember. I called it Cardboard City and it was always cold and scary, but I slept better there than in the children's home.

Sometimes I stayed out for a few nights before going back of my own volition. Other times a missing persons report was filed, and the police brought me back. But it got to the point where I had run away so many times that they didn't bother as much. And they certainly weren't interested in the reasons why I was doing it.

Occasionally a member of staff from Farmlands did a cursory sweep of the area and brought me back. Gary and Pauline did that a lot, and when either of those two came, I was happy to go with them, knowing I'd be safe. If Gary was on a twenty-four hour shift, I'd sleep well and when Pauline found me, we usually went back to her house for a while.

Every time I ran away, it created a mountain of paperwork, so it was common for some staff at Farmlands to leave it until the very last minute before reporting me missing to the police. They, in turn, would wait a good few hours before taking action. A missing child was something to deal with at the end of their night shift, when they'd call into Farmlands to collect a G71 form.

The G71 included a description of the child, what they were wearing, when they were last seen and where they might have gone. In theory, that information was distributed to other police on patrol to keep a look out. But to some officers, a missing care home kid was not a priority.

What was a priority to the police in the early 90s was something called TWOC-ing, which stands for Taking Without Owner's Consent. Basically, stealing a car and joyriding. It was rife, and higher on the list of importance because the youths stealing the cars were risking other's lives. And cars are valuable. To an over-stretched and under-resourced force, a child who regularly absconded from a care home was just a pain because to their mind, we were putting ourselves in danger on purpose.

When I ran away, my main aim was to keep out of sight of Brett, Carl and anyone else who might want to abuse me. But I couldn't stay in carboard city all the time, I had to eat. There was a man at the fish and chip shop who sometimes gave me a free bag of chips, or sometimes I'd beg for money or chalk drawings on the pavements for cash. There were many times though, where I wished to God that I'd not left the confines of my temporary den.

One time, Brett had noticed I'd been missing for a while and came looking for me. He wanted to put me to work to make himself some money and it didn't take long for him to find me.

'Hiding from me again, are you?'

He made me jump. I'd been making my way back to cardboard city, having had no luck with begging for food.

'No,' I lied, my stomach knotting.

'That's not what it looks like to me. And it looks like you're short of something to do, so you might as well get out there,' he said, pointing towards the edge of Victoria station. I had zero choice.

'Hurry up, I've seen someone who looks interested.'

I was cold, tired and hungry. The very last thing I wanted to do was go with a punter, but I took up my position as instructed. It didn't take long for a car to stop circling and come to a halt. He wound his window down and I saw his dark, menacing face.

'How much to wank me off?' he asked.

I told him the price and got into his car. Instead of him taking me to one of the usual spots, he drove only a very short distance, still within the city limits, to a run-down area where it looked like the houses were all built on top of each other, stacked one behind another and side by side. I think they were council flats. He parked up and told me to get out, said we were going inside because he didn't feel comfortable in the car.

I wish I'd made a run for it there and then.

It was quite disorientating because up close, all the flats looked the same, deprivation on every level. We got to a battered looking door, which he unlocked with a yale key. Then he shoved me inside and bolted it behind him. That's when I saw there was another man. He was about the same age as the guy who'd picked me up, mid-thirties with the same dark skin, but heavier-set. They weren't muscle-bound but I soon realised their strength.

The place was run down and dirty with rubbish everywhere, empty vodka bottles, over-flowing ashtrays and a heavy smell of cannabis. There was a huge bong in the centre of the room with bits of tin foil and abandoned dirty teaspoons. It was obviously some kind of drugs den. This was the first situation I'd been in where there was more than one man, and I was absolutely petrified.

It was unbearably traumatic, and I was kept there for two days. They did every sexual thing to me that you can imagine. It was prolonged, it was violent, and it was penetrative. It was extremely painful. I honestly thought I was going to die as they took it in turns to abuse me. When one finished, the other started again and all I could do was close my eyes and pray. I wasn't given anything to eat or drink and the only communication was between themselves or to aggressively bark orders about what they wanted me to do. I was in complete survival mode, forcing myself to feel nothing or think nothing. Too frightened to try and bring something else to mind to block it out. I wanted them to kill me so it would all be over.

On the second day, one of them passed out in the room next door. I was pretending to be asleep to avoid yet another assault from the other, when I heard him leave the flat. I kept completely still, my eyes and ears wide open to the small possibility that I might be able to get out of there. It was risky, particularly as I was so weak from all the abuse, but I realised it might be my only chance.

I thought I could sneak past without him noticing if he remained asleep or drugged, so I crept past as quickly and quietly as I could to reach the main door. My heart was pounding so hard as I reached for the latch and to my utter relief, it released. I peered through to check nobody was at the other side, then stepped out, leaving the door slightly ajar to prevent the latch clicking.

Then I bolted down a huge flight of stairs, through alleyways, past endless doors all looking the same, until finally, I saw the main entrance to the flats. Pausing for the smallest second to make sure the abuser wasn't on his way back in, I made a break for freedom.

It was bitterly cold. I ran as fast as I could to Victoria bus station, through the shopping centre, where I frantically begged for some bus money. My chest was in agony from gulping the freezing air. I must have looked utterly desperate because a kind soul gave me enough to get on the next bus to Top Valley, where I hid right at the back, slouching below the window. I was absolutely filthy, hugging my knees to my chest for warmth, praying that when I reached the stop nearest Farmlands, one of the kind members of staff would be on shift.

I carefully opened the door and spotted Gary and Rose in the communal area. I was in deep shock, but on seeing them, a sense of relief flooded through me. I knew I'd be alright for a while.

I didn't want anyone to catch me in that state. I was desperate to get clean and warm and dry and lay down on my bed to sleep, but Gary and Rose had clocked me and once I was out of earshot, they came up with a plan.

'He's staying here tonight. We're not letting him out. He's going nowhere,' said Gary.

'Agreed. Look at the state of the poor boy,' replied Rose.

Gary hovered outside the bathroom door as I showered and changed, making sure none of the other children came near me. Meanwhile, Rose made me a sandwich and a warm drink, which she brought up to my room. Rose sat on the end of my bed as I leant against the pillows to eat and drink. She didn't ask where I'd been, just stayed with me, probably guessing that I'd been forced to work in some kind of renting capacity. She had no idea of the true horror I'd faced.

Eventually, she left me to rest, but only a couple of hours later, through my bedroom window, I could see a car pulling up at the end of the drive. It was flashing its lights, beeping the horn. I couldn't see who was in it, but I feared the men in the flat had tracked me down.

I wanted to hide, but I was completely controlled by Brett and these unseen paedophile ring leaders. I had no say in my fate. If I didn't get back out there now, then it would only be a matter of time before they got me. I couldn't anger them further, so in my shocked and panicked state I felt I had more of a chance of survival if I faced the music. Gary and Rose obviously sensed my sudden panic when I started rushing around, getting dressed again. I was like a coiled spring, pacing around on high alert, mentally preparing myself. But when I got to the entrance of the door, Gary was stood in front of it.

'Nope,' he said.

But even though not one single part of me wanted to push past Gary, I felt I had no choice but to try. The consequences of me not getting out seemed to far outweigh those of staying. Using my elbows, my fists, anything I could, I fought with Gary to get out. Or rather, I tried to fight with Gary, but he didn't retaliate. He just stood dead still. 'You're not going,' said Rose, coming up behind me.

'I AM' I screamed.

'You can hit me, punch me, do what you like, but there is absolutely no way on earth that you are leaving this building tonight,' warned Gary.

My emotions were all over the place because of course I didn't want what was waiting for me at the other side of the door. I knew there would be trouble and pain. Gary and Rose could see that. They must have known I was only trying to escape through fear, so held strong, not once fighting me back, just firmly barring the door, letting me hit and punch and scream my frustration.

I'll never know if Gary and Rose's intervention saved my life that night, but in doing so, they should have been reported to management for restricting my civil liberties. They took the risk because they were in charge and had made a secret pact, putting their own jobs on the line to help me. I'll always be eternally grateful.

After trying and failing to get past them both, I eventually gave up. I was lucky that night because other staff members would have let me walk through the door to whatever fate awaited me. Gary guided me back to my bedroom, where he stayed and watched a *Star Trek* video with me, until he could see I was a bit calmer. He promised to stay outside my bedroom door all night to ensure I got a full night's sleep.

After that incident, Gary put himself in charge of shift rotas at Farmlands. Wherever possible, he ensured that either himself, Rose or Avril were always there, to make me feel safe. It meant all their shifts were harder because they couldn't work with each other, but my welfare was placed above their preferences and for a short while, my life was a bit better.

A few weeks later I was taken to the Genitourinury Medical (GUM) clinic after reporting blood and white puss coming out of my penis. I was convinced those two men had given me HIV. Tests were run and I'd caught something, but not HIV, so medicine was handed out and before long it was business as usual in every sense of the word.

Other than Gary's rota changes, no extra safety measures were put in place for me at Farmlands.

12

•

The Depths

I'D HIT the depths. I felt utterly hopeless.

Even with the support of Pauline and the play therapy with Anna, I couldn't see a way out. There was no chance of breaking this cycle until I was sixteen, when my place in the children's home would become void and another unlucky child would get my room and no doubt suffer the same fate.

I wondered what the least painful way would be to take my own life and it seemed that, without access to painkillers or other drugs, bleeding to death was the best option.

The moment came when I'd absconded yet again and had spent a couple of nights in cardboard city. Predictably, Brett found me, and I'd been made to go with various men in their cars, doing to them – or letting them do to me – whatever they wished.

Just before the last punter returned me back to base, I noticed the cover of a compact disc on the floor. It was a compilation of nursery rhymes. There was something about the pictures of Humpty Dumpty and Little Bo Beep that caught me off guard. This man had a toddler at home, yet here he was, with me.

Were all adults like this? Did they all have one side that was good and a darker, hidden side? When the saw me looking at the CD, I saw his shame as he handed me the cash.

This time, I decided I wasn't giving that money to Brett and asked the guy to drop me elsewhere. It was a good half mile away from Victoria station, near what looked like a disused building surrounded by wire fencing. I waited until he'd driven off then began searching for a sharp object, something to pierce my wrists with.

I was tearful but resolute. It wasn't that I wanted to be dead, I just didn't want to live this life anymore and saw no other way out. I spotted a loose piece of metal poking out from the fence and pulled at it to break it free. After a bit of twisting and turning I had the inch-long weapon in my hand, rough and sharp and ready to take me away from this hell.

Finding a spot round the corner and out of the way, I braced myself for the inevitable. Leaning back against the wall, I dragged the object across my left wrist, slowly and gently at first, almost like a dress rehearsal. I hadn't pierced the skin too deeply, more of a graze because it hurt like mad. I tried again, edging closer to the protruding veins. Pushing harder, I managed to go deeper, gouging a line from my wrist up towards my elbow, but I was surprised at how painful it was. In my head, I'd imagined it to be quick and only hurt for a short while, then I'd be in oblivion. But the pain was horrendous, and I burst into tears, cradling my arm.

I was suddenly shocked at what I'd tried to do and felt the need to be away from there, back at Farmlands, where somebody might fix me or help me. I wrapped part of my jumper around the wound to stop the flow then made my way back across the city to the bus stop, alert for Brett, who might now be wondering why I hadn't returned with his money.

The injury can't have been too bad, otherwise I'd have fainted with the loss of blood. And nobody seemed to be taking any notice or coming to my rescue as I waited at Victoria station – not even the bus driver, when I paid for my ticket. But if I'd been hoping for sympathy and care back at the children's home, I was sadly mistaken.

Unfortunately, neither Gary, Rose or Avril were on shift that day. When I walked in and showed a member of staff the state of my arm, I was met with an eye roll as if this was just another drama for them to deal with. An over-dramatic child looking for attention. I had no sense of being taken seriously over what had quite clearly been an attempt to take my own life.

They washed and patched the wound, then basically that was

the end of it for them. I wasn't asked why I had tried to take my own life or even offered any kind of follow up advice.

I still have the scar, but in my thirties, I had a tattoo done to cover it up. I didn't want to be constantly reminded of that time in my life when I was so low that I wanted to end it all.

13

•

A Little Love

MY PLAY therapy sessions were drawing to a close as Anna completed all the work needed for her degree. We had really bonded, and I knew I'd miss her a lot. I'd had a safe place to play, with someone kind, but she understood that for me to make any more progress, something drastic needed to change. She saw that I was barely getting through each day at Farmlands, never mind living a life where I could hope to thrive.

Anna was about twenty-three years old at the time and a colleague of hers, who was also aligned to my case as an educational psychologist, noticed how invested she was in my success. The two of them regularly discussed my progress after the sessions at Nottingham University and so eventually, her colleague just came out with it.

'Why don't you adopt him?' she said to Anna.

At first, Anna thought her colleague was joking, but a seed had been planted to help in some way. She still had more work to do career wise – going on to complete a three-year doctorate in clinical psychology – so couldn't commit to adopting. But Anna wanted to give me whatever stability she could, so thought about fostering, whereby all the social services teams would remain in place for me.

When Anna finally completed her master's degree, she approached Nottinghamshire County Council regarding foster care. She was initially concerned about the fact that she was not married and a lesbian, but those two factors had no impact on the process at all. She went through all the standard vetting procedures including interviews, criminal record checks etc. They even met her parents and Anna's lodger at her house in Burnley.

It was only a matter of months before Anna got the go-ahead and it was agreed that due to her doctorate work with the NHS being Tuesday to Friday, she would be in sole charge of me just over the weekends. So every Friday evening one of the staff at Farmlands drove me to her house in Burnley, then on Mondays (Anna's study day), she would return me back to Farmlands or drop me at school that morning.

I was so happy with this new framework of care, but strangely, I had no idea that I'd officially been fostered. That word was never mentioned to me, and it wasn't until very recently – when I began writing this book – that I found out. As a young boy, I thought Anna had simply agreed to look after me more often and I saw no reason to question that. Anna assumed it had been explained to me at the children's home. When we discussed the situation as adults, neither of us could believe that for all those years I never knew.

At the time, all I cared about was getting away from Farmlands as often as possible. With this new plan, I'd be with Anna for three nights over the weekend, then still have the two long sessions with Pauline during the week. If the good staff were on shift in the interim, then I'd be alright. There were pockets of peace.

The first time I went to Anna's house was amazing. She was renting a two-up, two-down, one bed terrace in Burnley. When I was there, Anna slept on the sofa so that I could have her proper bed. But shortly after, she bought her first house with two bedrooms and the spare room became mine for three nights a week. I always slept so well at Anna's house because I knew I was completely safe.

The situation was as new for Anna as it was for me. With no experience of caring for younger siblings, Anna was feeling her way with this fostering role. I have no recollection of ever feeling less than loved when I was with Anna or her family, so she must have done something right.

Most Friday nights we watched movies at her house and on

Saturdays, we'd usually have a day out. It must have been hard for Anna because my attention span was so limited. I remember an exciting trip to Sea Life in Blackpool, where you could spend hours looking at all the different ocean creatures. Anna says we were round in fifteen minutes despite my interest in fish. I was always asking what we were doing next, three steps ahead of right now.

On Sundays we'd often walk Anna's dog, Nell, in the countryside and one of our regular haunts was Hardcastle Crags near Hebden Bridge. I loved the freedom of running through the fields and woodland and splashing in puddles with Nell. It felt soothing and uplifting. Unconditional love. I enjoyed the responsibility of holding the lead and then making sure she had enough food and water when we got home. That grounding is probably why I became interested in working with dogs later on.

I really did become part of Anna's life and was soon assimilated into most aspects of it. She wrote songs and played the guitar in a folk/indie/Britpop band called Draw and her lodger Tom was a member of the band, so they often rehearsed at the house. I loved chatting to her friends in rooms filled with music.

Anna's parents also lived in Burnley, so we visited regularly and I was immediately made to feel like I belonged. They were Scottish, and to this day, their passion for their homeland remains ingrained in me. I adore anything from the Highlands and feel right at home there. Whenever Scotland play rugby now, I cheer for them just like I did with Anna's dad.

Her dad even gave me his old Scotland rugby shirt, which although I was touched by the sentiment, I never wore. I'm not a fan of secondhand clothes – a legacy from only having itchy, horrible, dirty things to wear when I was living with my mother.

Anna's friends and family showed me love in many ways – from simply accepting me and letting me be with them, to gifts like that shirt. One of Anna's pals gave me a box of Maltesers once, but I overheard Anna saying to her 'he'll be hyper with all that sugar running through his veins.' She wasn't wrong.

I was still only just thirteen, and this sudden surge of acceptance was sometimes hard to deal with. I didn't know how to accept love without strings attached. I wasn't used to people giving me things without expecting anything in return and always worried the scenario could end at any minute, that the love would stop, and I'd be fending for myself again.

There was an incident, which still fills me with shame. We were at one of Anna's friend's houses in Burnley and there was a wad of cash on a table. I felt an overwhelming urge to take it and run, so waited until Anna and her friend were busy chatting, then when they thought I was watching cartoons in the next room, I stole it and crept out.

I used the money to get myself to London, where I booked into a hotel for two nights on my own. I still don't really know why I did it. Perhaps it was because I wanted to avoid the inevitable at Farmlands on the Monday? Or maybe, once I'd left the house, I got scared and genuinely didn't know where to go? I could have quite simply seen a chance for adventure and taken it.

Anna was worried sick. She was in charge of me, and I'd disappeared without a trace. But she forgave me. She understood. But I wonder why no questions were asked at the hotel when a young boy turned up alone, with cash, requesting a room for a couple of nights?

One of Anna's fondest memories of fostering me was during a meal in a restaurant with a bunch of her colleagues. About twelve of them were all sat around a table, celebrating a milestone at work and I just mingled right in, chatting to the adults, holding court and charming everybody. As I did so, she sat back and watched the evening unfold, feeling proud of the way I was conducting myself.

'That's my boy,' she said.

Being dropped back at Farmlands after three nights with Anna always felt like a huge wrench. I was living two separate lives and some of the other children were jealous. One of them was Ian. One Monday after drop-off, he started bullying me as soon as I entered the building. It was all the usual jibes about being gay, rent-boy, that kind of thing, but for some reason, I couldn't take anymore and shouted back. But instead of punching me, he ran up to my bedroom and began trashing it.

The bed was tipped over, my curtains pulled off the rails, chair kicked, door punched, *Star Trek* and Madonna posters ripped down, TV wire yanked out of the socket. I was convinced that he'd empty my fish out too, so just stood there, balling my fists, letting let him go wild. It was all I could do. I was trying my hardest not to cry tears of frustration, but inevitably, they began falling down my cheeks.

'Oh, look at the cry baby,' he jeered in my face. 'What's wrong? Don't you want me to touch your precious things?'

I snapped.

'Leave me alone. Get out,' I yelled.

'Why's that then? I heard you liked having boys in your bedroom.'

I saw red. I was sick of him ruining all my things, calling me names. This wasn't the first time he'd trashed my room, just the first time I'd seen him do it.

I went wild, properly kicking seven bells out of him, my anger pouring out of every punch to his body and face. I wanted to hurt him as badly as he'd hurt me, as badly as Brett and all the other men had hurt me. In that moment, I became unaware of who I was hitting. I just knew I needed to keep punching and punching. The fury was animalistic, momentum building until I realised he was backing off, edging out of the door while two staff members ran towards the mayhem.

They saw the state of my bedroom. They took in the fact that Ian had a bloodied lip and ripped T-shirt. And they saw me, smaller than Ian, back to the wall, slipping down, with a scraped face and torn trousers. I looked up, expecting another tirade of verbal abuse for fighting. But to my surprise, one of them grabbed Ian and marched him away, and the other began silently putting my room back together around me. Nothing else was said about the incident. Perhaps they sensed I'd reached the end of my tether – or felt Ian had it coming.

When Pauline arrived the next day after school, she asked me why my cheek was swollen. I told her what happened, and though she didn't agree with violence at all, I think she accepted my retaliation for what it was. The staff urged Pauline to take me to the cinema – to take my mind off it – and though she usually preferred us doing more wholesome activities, she saw my need to zone out and we went to see *Free Willy*.

There was something about that movie that resonated with me. I was rapt throughout the whole thing and even sat still. Perhaps it was because the whale needed to be rescued, or maybe because I was about the same age as the young boy who helped the whale escape. As soon as it came out on video, Pauline bought it and kept it at her house, so I could watch it whenever I wanted, without fear of one of the children at Farmlands finding and stealing it.

When Pauline drove me home that evening, I pointed out the road where my grandma and grandad lived.

'Have you not seen them in a while?', Pauline asked.

'I'm not allowed to see them,' I answered.

'Why not?'

'I don't know, they won't tell me.'

Pauline didn't say anything and kept driving back to Farmlands. But I could tell she was as confused as me regarding access.

I was expecting my bedroom to have been trashed again, but when I reached the door, everything was still in place. Brett was nowhere to be seen and all I could hear was Tim in his bedroom opposite, dancing to Michael Jackson's *Thriller*.

I put my own headphones on, clicked play on my Sony Walkman and turned the volume up on a mixtape Gary had made for me. We had different tastes, but he included a few he knew I liked, such as Alison Moyet's 'Is This Love?' and 'Where Hides Sleep'.

This was my life. A rollercoaster hurtling between the highs of time spent with Anna or Pauline and despairing lows of waiting to be forced into earning money for Brett and Carl. It was particularly tough when other children had family visits at Farmlands because my family had disowned me. I'd watch their excitement building, then their sadness after they'd gone. But at least their parents bothered. Small acts of kindness like Gary's mix-tapes helped, even though they were frowned upon by management because staff weren't meant to get emotionally involved.

Pauline must have been mulling over the fact that I wasn't supposed to see my grandparents, because when she collected me from Farmlands as usual a couple of days later, we took a detour.

'Can you remember exactly where grandma and grandad live?'

I could. I knew exactly which street and house number.

'Yes,' I said.

'Would you like to go and see them?' she asked.

I really did want to, but I knew I shouldn't.

'I'm not allowed, Pauline. The social workers say I've not to.'

Pauline said that if I could direct her to where they lived, then she'd see if we could go in. From her front passenger seat, I pointed left, right, round corners and through traffic lights until eventually, we pulled up outside their council house. Pauline couldn't believe how close it was to Farmlands and that in all this time nobody had travelled the short distance to take me there.

The house hadn't changed a bit from the outside. Same pebbledash, just more run down. The grass seemed longer than I remembered, and the black paint on the gate was warped and peeling off. 'Come on then,' Pauline said, unbuckling her seatbelt, 'let's see what they've got to say.'

It was at least six years since I'd last seen them, so I wasn't sure what to expect. But when Pauline knocked and my grandma came to the door, she looked so happy. She couldn't believe it was me, right there on her doorstep. I'd grown a lot taller in the intervening years, so when she recovered herself and leaned in to hug me, she didn't even need to stoop. That was a great hug. As her arms enveloped me, I looked over at Pauline and saw her wide smile. I didn't know what to do with my arms or have any idea what to say, so I just enjoyed the moment.

'Hi, Grandma.'

'It's you, after all this time,' she said.

'Can we come in?' Pauline asked.

'Of course. Come on.'

Grandad appeared from the lounge when he heard the conversation.

'You shouldn't really be here,' he said, making his way to a chair at the kitchen table.

'Well, he's here now, so let's see him,' said Grandma.

We sat in the kitchen for about forty-five minutes and in all that time, Grandma wouldn't let go of my hand. I could feel her love and warmth as she asked me all about where I was living and what it was like. I told her I didn't like staying at Farmlands, but that Pauline was nice, and I spent weekends with Anna. I wanted to ask if I could stay with her, but something about my Grandad's demeanour stopped me.

The inside of her house hadn't changed one bit. There were still hundreds of trinkets from Blackpool, along with picture postcards of the tower pinned to the walls. It was like stepping back in time. It even smelled the same – that comforting aroma of meat and potatoes cooking in the oven and a fusty smell, unique to pensioners.

Time went too quickly, but when Grandad said we had to go, Pauline sensed there was no use arguing. She stood up and said how lovely it had been to meet them and that if they didn't mind, she would bring me back again. Grandma agreed but grandad still hung back. We had one last hug and then she waved us off from her doorstep. It had been so great to see her. I loved her. My Grandma was kind, and she was family. As we drove away, I felt hopeful that we'd be able to go again because I wanted her in my life as much as possible.

Pauline got into trouble for that visit and was hauled into the office. Word had reached my mother.

'What do you think about smacking, Pauline?' the manager at Farmlands asked her.

Before she had chance to answer, he cut in again.

'Because that's the reason he isn't allowed to see his grandparents. They smack him.'

Pauline couldn't believe what she was hearing. She'd seen firsthand the love in my grandma's eyes during that visit and felt sure it wasn't true. But this was Pauline's job, she needed the income and didn't want to jeopardise our visits, so grudgingly apologised.

'Do not go again,' he said.

'We won't.'

I was also told off for letting her take me.

Pauline and I both suspected that my mother had rung Farmlands when she found out about the visit, then lied about the smacking, because I don't think Grandma or Grandad ever hit me. My mother still had the last word about who I could and couldn't see for my own 'safety'. I knew her though. The only reason she prevented me from seeing the rest of the family was to hurt me, to punish me for being gay. It was all she had while I wasn't under her roof.

I saw my dad just once more while I was living at Farmlands, when I was collected by surprise from school. I was at a special school in Billborough. I don't know why they put me there, but it seemed standard procedure for a lot of looked-after children. I didn't enjoy it, but at least when I was in a classroom, I was left alone.

Concentration was a huge problem for me in lessons because there was always so much else going on in my life. I couldn't see the point of spellings when my day-to-day existence was so haphazard. If adults didn't care enough to protect me from paedophiles, how bothered were they, really, that I knew the difference between *there* and *their*?

But one morning after registration, I was called to the office. My step-brother Dale (my dad's wife's son from her previous marriage) had arrived to take me to see my dad. It was totally unexpected. He just introduced himself and off we went. I'd never met him before but had no reason to believe this tall skinny sixteen-year-old with light brown hair and smiley eyes wasn't who he said he was.

It was only about fifteen minutes on foot to my dad's house, so I walked next to him all the way there. I didn't ask too many questions because I was just pleased to be getting out of class and excited about this chance to see my dad again. It had been about a year since I visited him with Pauline, and I wasn't sure why he wanted another reunion. Last time, he made it clear he believed I'd abused Claire.

This time, I was allowed inside. What a mess. Considering he'd been expecting me, there had been no effort to tidy up or run a duster round the place. It felt chaotic, like I'd been dumped into the middle of a *Mad Max* movie. He lived there with his wife, her three children from her previous marriage, and another three children which they'd had together.

'This is Dawn' he said, introducing me to his wife.

I didn't get a great feeling about Dawn. It's not that she was particularly mean, but she wasn't welcoming either. She was short with a squashed nose and quite ugly – and she wasn't very clean. Then I met Jared, another step-brother, about the same age as me. He looked similar to Dale but had a bit more of his mother in him. Jared was not a nice person, and I could tell he didn't want me there, going out of his way to intimidate me.

I stayed for a few hours. We didn't do anything special, just sat around and talked before Dale took me back to school. It was a weird experience and I never understood why I'd been invited. Had the penny finally dropped that I had nothing to do with Claire? It can't have just been curiosity. The next time I saw my dad was by pure coincidence – an event which left me in complete turmoil.

14

•

Disbelieved

IT'S HARD for me to put into words just how controlling Brett and Carl were. Everything I did with them sexually was because it was the lesser of two evils.

For Brett particularly, it was all about power. He engineered situations to make it look like I was abusing *them*, or at least consenting, so that if I ever complained, I wouldn't be believed.

I was laid on my bed with my eyes closed listening to Alison Moyet on my Walkman. Her lyrics always spoke to me, especially 'Invisible' and 'All Cried Out'. But then I sensed movement and my eyes shot open as Carl yanked my headphones off my ears.

'Let's go outside,' he said.

Oh God.

'I don't want to,' I dared to defy.

'Brett says,' he replied, glaring at me.

That was that then. If I didn't go, he'd only come and find me and make whatever he was planning to do a lot worse. I swung my legs off the bed and stood up. Looking out of the window I could see it was drizzling and already getting dark for an early September evening, but I didn't have time to grab a jumper or coat. Carl just shoved me out of the door and frog-marched me down the corridor.

When we got to the main door, he told me to act casual walking past staff, then led me around the corner to the grounds outside. I was casting my eyes around, wondering where Brett was, expecting him to jump out at any minute and assault me. I could feel the light rain on the back of my neck and the grass was damp underfoot, making my trainers squeak. Carl pushed me to the end of the garden, where brambles and bushes about a metre thick lined the boundary.

Brett emerged from the shrubbery and smiled grimly at Carl. He started to undo his trousers and it became clear what he was after. Oral sex. If I did it without resistance, that might be all I had to do. If I tried to get away, I'd be submitting myself to a beating and inevitable submission in the end. It was a lose-lose situation, especially as by this point, I'd already made numerous complaints to staff and police about him and Carl – and nothing had changed.

I just got on with it, blanking out the hideous smell of him, moving as fast as I could to get it over with, while Carl looked on.

Finally, it was over. I spat out his cum and wiped my mouth on my arm.

'Since Carl went to all the trouble of fetching you, I think he deserves something too,' said Brett.

No. Not again.

'He wants bumming, so you'd better get on with it before someone sees we're here.'

I stepped back, reflexively, but Brett quickly pulled out a knife and pointed the tip at my throat. I gulped.

'Which part of that didn't you understand?' he growled into my face.

'Sorry. Yes, I understand.'

He held my stare for a few seconds then laughing, stepped back and wiped the blade on his sleeve. I understood.

I despised Carl as much as I hated Brett – and this act involved a lot more pressure. It's not easy trying perform when that very act is the last thing you want to do. They had no condoms either, giving the whole scenario an added level of fear and danger. The only way I could hope to do what he wanted was by forcing myself to think of someone else. I tried my best to imagine someone in a boyband, but it just wasn't working.

Later that night, Brett played his trump card. To make my other claims against him seem invalid, he told staff that he'd caught me 'bumming' Carl. To further his case, he pressured another kid at Farmlands to say he'd witnessed the same incident. Brett's claims were taken seriously and a few days later I was interviewed by the police about it.

It was horrible being treated like a criminal. A member of staff from Farmlands took me to the station – and it wasn't one of the kind ones. I sensed they thought I had this coming to me, as though this is what I deserved for my deviant behaviour. Their homophobia was blatant.

We were taken through to an interview room and I was told that whatever I said was being recorded and could be used as evidence against me. The solicitor they provided for me urged me to keep saying 'no comment' whenever I was asked a question. But 'no comment' didn't sit right with me. Why should I say that, when I had plenty to comment on? I wanted to tell the truth as much as I could. As much as I dared.

'Is it true that you tried to have penetrative sex with Carl in the grounds of Farmlands three days ago?' the policeman asked.

'Yes,' I replied.

I wanted them to know that I'd been forced into it, that I was fully in the clutches of both Brett and Carl, and if I'd tried to get out of the situation, my fate would have been worse. Brett had a knife, for God's sake. This felt like my one chance to set the record straight and let someone else in authority know what had been going on all this time – because staff at Farmlands so far had done nothing to help me.

The police already knew I had been abused by paedophiles in Nottingham because there are records of it. I'd been picked up by police for loitering around the men's toilets or bus station numerous times. In fact, it was often a relief to be caught because even though I felt the officers saw me as a nuisance, they did sometimes give me a Cup-a-Soup or a sandwich. And I was sheltered in a cell until someone from Farmlands collected me or an on-duty social worker with the police took me back.

Yet they still chose to believe that I was renting my body because I wanted to. I told them repeatedly at the time that I was forced to do it, to earn money for someone else, but they seemed to take the view that that's what all gay men did, that it was part and parcel of what being homosexual meant.

In this interview room I didn't feel I was being listened to in any way – by the police, by the solicitor or by the member of staff from Farmlands. It was like nobody was interested in the background to why I had ended up in this nightmare situation.

All they wanted to focus on was that one specific act with Carl. That's what I was at the station for, nothing else. I felt pushed, pressured into admitting that I'd tried to penetrate Carl, even though I told them I hadn't wanted to do it, that I was coerced. The way they spoke to me, their tone, the body language, all just screamed homophobia.

I could tell that the solicitor and staff member at Farmlands were cross with me for not sticking to their plan of me saying 'no comment'. For them, it meant more of a headache. I sensed that they – along with the police – were cringing at some of the details, more horrified by the thought of a homosexual act than the fact I was being systematically abused. Their focus was all wrong.

In the end, the policeman conducting the interview decided to caution me for buggery there and then. Something which remains on my criminal record. He didn't want to concern himself with the coercion side of things. He couldn't be bothered to action an investigation to get to the truth. Basically, he didn't do his job properly. As far as I know, neither Brett nor Carl were reprimanded for the incident.

I often wonder if it had been a girl in my situation, would the police have acted differently? Would they, the staff and solicitor have understood that a young girl didn't want to be pimped by older men in Nottingham or forced into sexual acts by others in the children's home? I suspect it would have been a different case entirely.

A whole two months later, there was a strategy meeting at Farmlands to discuss a plan for my safety. They were looking at a long-term residential placement for me elsewhere, but in the end settled for an unworkable scheme where I was to be supervised all day, every day. Less than eight weeks later, they admitted this hadn't been possible due to staff shortages. Nottinghamshire County Council investigated whether I was at risk from paedophiles, male adults and peers, but they chose not to place me on the 'At Risk' register.

There's a photocopy of a letter I left at Farmlands round about this time. It says, 'I have gone and am never coming back because I hate being called rent boy or batty boy.' I ran away for the umpteenth time, distressed, unhappy and hoping for any chance of escape.

For the next few nights, I lived in carboard city again. The weather was turning colder and keeping warm was hard. I was surviving off bits of cash from begging until Brett came looking for me. This was the last time he put me to work though, as something happened which neither of us had seen coming.

At the back of the Victoria Shopping Centre was a disused furniture warehouse on an old industrial unit. It was really grim. There was smashed glass and drug-use paraphernalia all over the place and it stank of human waste. It was on two levels and upstairs a dirty mattress lay on the floor. A place where addicts got their highs, rough sleepers dossed, and paedophiles got their kicks.

Brett knew this was a good place for business, but it always felt scarier that our usual haunts. That's where he wanted to go that night though, so that's where we went and after about twenty minutes waiting in the cold, he spotted a potential punter. The guy looked to be in his early thirties, white, quite short but strong, like he lifted weights – and was pacing around like a caged animal, ready to attack. I knew he was going to be my next job.

'Go and see what he wants,' said Brett.

By this point in my life, I had a good gauge of who was dangerous and who was just perverted. This guy looked like he was both. 'Whatever he asks for, give it to him. You'll need the money to buy something for me later.'

I walked over and as soon as I saw the look in his eyes, I knew this was going to be brutal. We agreed on oral sex, I told him the price and we disappeared inside the industrial unit. As usual, I thought to myself that as soon as I get it over with, the better. And with Brett stood outside, I could hardly say no.

Richie – Who Cares?

'Get upstairs,' barked the guy, pushing me towards the step.

I couldn't see the point in going upstairs if he was just after a blow job, but he wasn't the sort of person to argue with, so I did as I was told. He was right behind me, pushing my back, so close I could smell his cheap cider breath. At the top of the stairs, he pushed me harder, towards the dirty mattress and began to undo his trousers. 'Lie down on your front,' he shouted.

'But you said you wanted oral. I can't do that if I'm lying down,' I replied.

'Shut the fuck up and do what I say. Lie the fuck down'

He pushed me so hard that I had to break my fall with my elbows, and before I had chance to scramble back up, he'd laid on top of me, pressing me down, and was tugging at my trousers, yanking them to my thighs as his breathing grew stronger. I tried to wriggle away. This wasn't what we'd agreed.

'Don't,' I shouted as I could feel him trying to force his cock into me.

There was little chance of Brett coming to my rescue and no hope of this man stopping what he was about to do. He was so violent, clawing and scratching me with his grubby hands. I was absolutely trapped beneath him as he rammed himself into me again and again – each time it was pure agony, like a hot knife searing through me.

I was crying in pain and begging him to stop but he was zoned into what he wanted. I squeezed my eyes closed and held my breath, forcing my face into the mattress to muffle my screams and drown the noise of his guttural moans.

I felt physically and mentally broken when he pulled himself out and fastened his trousers. I curled into a ball as he stood up and threw some notes in my direction. Then laughing, he strode off down the steps.

I waited until I couldn't hear him anymore then pulled my trousers up and limped my way downstairs. It had been terrifying. I wondered how badly he'd injured me internally and prayed to God that he wasn't HIV positive. Brett appeared around the corner, arms wrapped around himself against the cold.

'You took your time. Where's my money?'

I handed him the cash and stuffing it in his pocket, he told me to follow him. I felt like a zombie, blindly traipsing behind him, shivering at the sheer desperation of everything. Right then, I didn't want to live a moment longer.

Brett wanted to get high on lighter fluid, but his face was infamous in the area and some shops refused to serve him. His plan was for us both to get in a cab and to go to a few different petrol stations.

'Tell them your mum sent you in a taxi to get it' he said.

We sat side by side in the back seat of a cab in Nottingham. Him, itching for a fix. Me, freezing cold, exhausted and in pain.

We pulled up at the first station and I made my way inside. I looked a state. God knows what the person on the till must have thought – or the taxi driver. But I did as Brett said and reeled off the lie. For added authenticity, he wanted me to wave at the driver as I was being served, to make it look like he knew that everything was alright.

One canister wasn't enough for Brett though and we had to go to two more petrol stations, repeating the scam. I wondered why the taxi man thought it was okay for a thirteen-year-old boy to be buying cans of lighter fluid. Why hadn't he seen what was happening and driven us straight to the police station?

Brett instructed the driver to drop us back in the city centre and, paying him with the money I'd been through hell to earn for him, got out.

For a split second, I thought that was me done for the night. I stayed still, wondering if there was any chance I could be driven back to Farmlands, where I could sleep, knowing that Brett was elsewhere.

But Brett put his face right up to the window.

'Come on. Get out,' he snarled.

He wanted to get high, and I had to go with him.

In the old market square on Long Row was Habitat, Next and RJ's. At the side of that, an alleyway to Hertz Yard joined onto it from underneath the main road. He wanted to get on top of the flat roof. I followed him, grabbing a shutter on one side of the alley, and pulling myself into a position so each foot was either side of the wall. Then we shimmied up onto a low roof where metal fire escape steps led to a higher, bigger roof. That was Brett's chosen spot for getting off his face that night.

I had absolutely no idea why he wanted to be up there when there were plenty of hidden corners at ground level in the city. We were even more exposed to the elements, with only about a metre high wall surrounding the roof, barely shielding the biting wind. Looking out, you could see large swathes of the city, shops now closed for the evening, lights off, everyone home.

Pieces of rubbish gusted around the roof – cigarette butts, dirty carrier bags and a squashed pile of old cardboard boxes in one of the corners.

'I'm freezing Brett,' I dared to say. 'Can't you do this somewhere else?'

I still didn't know why he wanted me with him. He'd got his loot. Maybe he was after something sexual but surely, even he must have seen I was fit for nothing.

'Stop complaining,' he shouted, taking a suck on the first cannister of lighter fluid.

The thought of getting high on that stuff made me gip. I once tried a small amount under peer pressure and hated every minute. It gave me sharp pains in my chest which frightened the life out of me, and I swore I'd never do it again. I began jumping up and down to keep warm, blowing into my hands, hugging myself, anything I could think of to keep out the cold.

'Here, this'll keep you warm,' he said.

Brett picked up another canister and sprayed fluid all over the pile of cardboard and reached for the matches in his pocket. Looking right at me, he struck one and flung it toward the pile. The whooshing sound and sudden brightness took me aback, and though it was tempting to move towards the warmth, this felt too dangerous. What had he done? I stared at the flames throwing out black smoke, blowing this way and that as if looking for something else to envelop.

'Shit Brett, why've you done that?' I shouted

He thought it was hilarious. He was off his face, whirling around, yelling, head thrown back, whooping and cheering.

'That warm enough for you?' he shouted, squirting more fluid onto the fire.

I jumped back, frightened. The fire started creeping towards one of the wooden air vent casings and I knew once that was alight, we were in real trouble. It took hold so quickly, growing as manic as Brett in no time at all. I should have stayed and tried to quell the flames and wish so badly now that I'd at least tried. But there was nothing to put them out with. No extinguishers or fire blankets, nothing to beat it down.

I ran. I headed straight back the way we'd come, taking a leap onto the low roof, then shimmying down the sides of the walls until my foot reached the shutter. I dared not look back to see if Brett was following. For once, I was more scared of something else than him. I didn't want to be the next thing the flames found, I wanted to be as far away as possible.

Sliding the last couple of metres down, I managed to take off the top layer of skin on the insides of both of my arms and hands, but I didn't register the pain until much later. On solid ground, I pelted out of the alleyway, round the corner and stopped for just a few seconds to catch my breath and think. I could hear Brett following, trainers scraping down the brickwork and I knew I had to get away from him too, as fast as I could.

My head was spinning. This was an absolute nightmare. I hadn't even wanted to be there in the first place and now here I was, fleeing from what could be a major fire and Brett, who was totally off his head. I knew I had to ring the fire service because there was no way that fire was going to put itself out. But I was frightened of what would happen when I rang. They'd know I was there and think it was me. Brett would probably lie and tell them I started it – and with nobody else up there, I had no witnesses.

Looking up, I could see smoke rising, low flames spreading across the roof. Then I thought – what if someone's in there? Panic was really setting in now and I knew couldn't just run away from it.

Richie – Who Cares?

I had to get to the nearest phone box and dial 999. Because the layout of the city was so familiar to me, I headed straight for the nearest booth and rang. But before I could tell them what was happening, a drunk man reached in and started wrestling the receiver off me, shouting that I was lying, that it was a malicious call.

'It's not. It's true' I yelled, but he pushed me out of the way and slammed the phone down.

By this point, a few people were beginning to gather, wondering what the commotion was, looking skywards towards the roof where the fire was really taking hold. Someone, somehow, must have got through to the fire brigade though because eventually, I could hear sirens roaring closer as the blaze licked through the top floor windows.

I was stuck in the centre of this major drama unfolding before me, frozen in every sense of the word. I watched as fire engines pulled up and teams began unreeling the hoses and taking orders from their boss. But Brett, still totally high, started trying to get involved, running around the firemen, grabbing the hoses and causing an obstruction, drawing attention to himself.

His stupidity brought me to my senses, so while he was causing chaos, I saw that as my chance to escape. Nobody was paying any attention to a scruffy little teenager amid the furore, so it was easy to slip away.

When I walked back through the door of Farmlands, I acted as casually as I could. 'He's back,' I heard one of the staff say through the open office door.

I didn't hang around to explain myself and nobody rushed to check if I was alright.

'You been out renting again?' one of them called as I made my way to my bedroom.

It seemed to make no odds to them that I'd returned. News hadn't reached them about a fire in the city centre – and I certainly wasn't going to tell them.

Carl was nowhere to be seen. He might have gone out looking for Brett – hoping he'd have some money from my labours.

But whatever he was doing, it was good for me that he wasn't there – one less person for me to dodge, because right then, I just didn't have any fight left in me.

For all my exhaustion and exertion, the physical invasion and lack of food and warmth, I still wanted a shower before anything else. I needed to wash everything away from the past few days, rid myself of the stench of that mattress in the derelict building and the paedophile's spit clinging to my neck. There was smoke in my hair and dirt in my nails. My clothes and shoes unwashed, unchanged for days.

I would love to have been able to stay in the bathroom longer, but I never knew who might be lurking. There was no chance of waiting until the whole place steamed up to feel warm right through. I couldn't stand there with hot water cascading over my head, watching the suds and grime swirl down the plughole. That luxury was reserved for other kids who weren't bullied, who weren't gay. I quickly jumped in, lathered up as best I could, then rinsed, dressed and dashed over to my room. I could never have risked walking from bathroom to bedroom in just my towel for fear of people saying I was *asking for it*.

There was no Gary, Rose or Avril on duty, so I pushed a chair up under my door handle, quickly sprinkled some fish food in the bowl and laid down on top of my bed. My head was so crowded with the last few days' events that every time I began drifting off, images of the fire plagued my thoughts. I envisaged people trapped and dying, I saw Brett preventing stretchers from being loaded onto an ambulance, and Carl's face melting in the flames, sneering at me.

I must have snatched a couple of hours sleep because I was jolted awake by the noise of a fight happening further down the corridor. I seized the opportunity to sneak out, quickly swinging by the kitchen to grab some biscuits from the cupboard with the broken lock, stuffing one into my mouth and three others in my pocket. Because the staff were focused on the ruckus in the corridor, I dipped into the office and took the price of a day rider for the bus from the desk drawer, which they would have given me away anyway.

I headed right back to the scene of the fire, desperate to know if there had been any casualties, out of my mind thinking someone had been injured or killed.

What I saw was utter devastation. An entire block of shops in Nottingham city centre was decimated. All because Brett wanted to get high, and I wanted to be warm. It was too much to take in. The smell of wet, burned timber and melted plastic hung in the air, wisps of smoke still spiraling up through the debris.

It was cordoned off with official tape and surrounded by police keeping guard. I could see a couple chatting to a bobby nearby and slowly made my way over, hoping to catch what was being said. But the conversation had wound up by the time I reached them, so I waited a while and then stood near the policeman myself.

'Was anyone hurt?' I asked, not introducing myself.

'No casualties, thank God. Not that we know of anyway. Shopping centre had shut for the night so there were no customers or staff. Anyone who shouldn't have been in there must have got out because we've had no reports of bodies or remains as of yet.'

It was like he was reeling off a script to me, like I was one of the journalists from *The Nottingham Post* or local BBC Radio who'd been there earlier. A lot of people were interested in what had happened.

Then the policeman gave me more of a sideways glance, an up and down to see if he could believe his eyes.

The previous night, when police caught Brett for disturbing the firemen, they asked him what he knew. Brett told them that he'd been with me, and I'd started the fire because I was cold. He described what I'd been wearing, including the coat I had on right then. The policeman put his left hand on my shoulder and with his right hand, reached for his radio and spoke to base.

'Young man beside me wearing a coat of the same description we're after.'

I knew I was done for. My initial thought was to run, but his grip tightened as he looked at me. There was a reply from the other end of the radio, hard to understand through the crackles, but the gist was that he needed to get me to the station.

'Roger that. Over'

With one deft move, the policeman ended the discussion, grabbed his handcuffs and attached them to my wrists in front of my body. My stomach lurched.

'But I didn't' start it. It wasn't my fault. I tried to put it out, but it was spreading too fast, so I rang the fire brigade,' I protested.

'Right' he replied, unconvinced, linking his arm through mine.

'I swear, it wasn't me. I swear.'

Passers-by were homing in on events. They saw the cuffs and my protestations and put two and two together, talking amongst themselves, murmuring and pointing. This was a nightmare. I could see the huge amount of damage and disruption caused by the fire, and even though I didn't start it, I was there. Who was going to believe I had nothing to do with it? Especially if Brett was already at the station, twisting the truth to his advantage, placing the blame on me.

'Move aside please,' the policeman said to the crowds.

We needed to head towards the curb, and when he started walking, I saw no point in resisting. I'd followed worse men in my time.

A police car pulled up and the policewoman in the front passenger seat got out and immediately opened the back door, signaling for us to get in.

'Don't try anything stupid,' she said.

I felt stupid enough for having been dragged into this mess in the first place, so I wasn't about to make the situation worse. With the policeman behind me to block any chance of escape, I maneuvered myself in. He leaned over, clicked the seatbelt in and slammed the door, then quickly made his way to the other side to get in next to me.

The driver turned around and looked at me with disgust, like I was utter scum. This really did feel like the beginning of the end. Last night, I'd been side by side in the back of a taxi with Brett. Less than twenty-four hours later I was seated in a police car, on my way to the station.

The policewoman in front was asking me all the essential

details – my name, age, where I lived, who was in charge of me. She radioed this information ahead so somebody from Farmlands could get to the station as soon as possible. I would need a solicitor too, which they provided initially. I had no idea if I was going to be leaving the station again or whether this was it, I was going to jail.

So far, my experience of the authorities taking me seriously had been limited. Out of all the abuse I'd suffered at the hands of my peers and paedophiles, only one man had been brought to justice. I'd been cautioned for buggery with Carl without any further investigation as to why I'd been forced into the situation. Nobody had listened properly when I was being exploited at Willowdene by Kevin. I was just a kid from a children's home, causing trouble, with no chance of changing.

My head fell to my chest, and I slumped in the seat, feeling utterly hopeless and completely alone.

15

•

A Safer Place

I KNEW THE procedure. Interview room, desk, recorder. Police officer, member of staff from Farmlands, solicitor warning me to say, 'no comment.'

'Are you going to tell us what happened last night then?' was the opening gambit from the copper.

At this point, I wished I'd told the whole, absolute truth, and it still gnaws at me that I didn't. I just thought I had nothing to lose, that they wouldn't know either way, and it would make me look a bit better, perhaps get me off the hook.

No chance.

I told them exactly what had happened, then added a bit. I said I was forced into being with Brett, that he'd made me get the lighter fluid for him, that I had no option because of how he'd threatened me and that following him onto the roof was better than being beaten up or abused by him. But I also added that once the fire had started, I tried to put it out. And that was a lie.

I just panicked. I was only thirteen.

Should I have tried to put the fire out? What with? Could I have refused Brett and not bought him the lighter fluid? As if. What about when I was in the taxi – should I have told the driver? Or could I have grassed to the till operator at the petrol station? All these missed moments swirled around in my head.

Statement taken, I was released and driven back to Farmlands by a social worker. It was a very quiet journey. I wasn't asked any more questions and I offered up no excuses. By the time we reached the home, word had spread, and the children were all revved up because for once, something interesting had happened. The incident was on the news.

But there was another reason why they were happier – Brett wasn't there and was unlikely to be back for a very long time. He'd been arrested at the scene after causing a disturbance with the fire service, and because he was sixteen or just over, I think they kept him in or moved him somewhere secure. But I didn't care where he was, as long as he wasn't at Farmlands.

None of the nice staff were on shift so I couldn't talk to anyone about it. I walked right past all the other children and went straight to my room. Nobody bothered me that night. Staff seemed on high alert, perhaps fearful that the spotlight was suddenly on Farmlands, and they might be investigated. Even the tough kids – Carl and the other older ones – left me alone. Perhaps there was kudos attached to what they perceived I'd done. Maybe they thought they'd better not mess with me anymore in case I gave details about their bullying and abuse.

A member of staff was positioned outside my bedroom door all night, which at least meant I had the chance of some sleep. But nobody told me what the possible outcome might be or when the case might go to court. I was still hoping that they'd believe me, that Brett would go to prison, and I'd be spared.

The next morning, things weren't any clearer. School was off the agenda in case I tried to abscond, so I just waited in my room until Gary's shift started.

He knocked on my door and came in.

'Oh, what happened?'

My chin stared trembling. He was the first kind face I'd seen since the incident. I hadn't realised how much I'd been holding everything in – a ball of tension and fear, trying to keep myself together.

I told him what I'd told the police, including the part about me trying to put the fire out. But the difference was, Gary believed every word. He knew there was no way I'd have bought lighter fluid for myself, gone onto a roof and set some carboard on fire. Gary knew how manipulative Brett could be and how afraid I was of him.

Instead of having a go at me for being so stupid, for getting embroiled in this mess, he just sat down next to me, and we talked about what might happen next. Then it hit me that not only would Rose and Avril know about this, but my link worker Pauline, and my foster mum Anna. I felt I'd really let them down and knew that this situation was going to create stress for all of them.

A date was set for trial, 4th February 1997. In the interim, staff at Farmlands were meant to be monitoring me closely – almost on a one-to-one basis, but just like the last time they tried this approach, it failed due to lack of human resources. There were concerns that I'd run away, so Rose took matters into her own hands. After about a week of trying, she found somewhere safer, a place where the outside world couldn't get me, and I'd be protected from other children.

The place was called Aycliffe Young People's Centre in Newton Aycliffe, County Durham. Its where vulnerable under-sixteens can be kept safe (under Section 25 of the Children's Act, 1989). Rose said it was the best option until we knew the outcome of the trial, so even though I was nervous about a completely new environment, I was relieved that after all these years, my safety was finally a priority.

I didn't have chance to speak to Anna before my move, which I found very hard. But part of me assumed I'd be back after the trial, when it had been proven that Brett was guilty, and I was there only by coercion. It was very important to me that both she and Pauline knew I hadn't started the fire. I wasn't the sort of person who caused unnecessary damage to property, and I had no previous record of arson, unlike Brett.

I managed to briefly see Pauline before I was taken to Aycliffe.

'I didn't start the fire, Pauline. It wasn't me, it was Brett. It was freezing, we were cold, he made me go and get the lighter fluid and that's what he lit it with. He lit it because I said I was cold,' I told her.

'I know, I know,' she soothed.

She believed me, I knew she did. Pauline was fully aware of Brett's control, but I could tell how sad she was. We both knew that Aycliffe was over two hours' drive away, which meant we wouldn't be able to see each other much while I was there. That was one of the hardest things to take in.

Once Rose got the green light, everything moved quickly, and I was told to pack as much as I could fit into one suitcase. As Pauline was there, she helped me fill it with clothes, my Walkman, various C90 cassettes, my *Star Trek* posters and duvet cover. I put a couple of my favourite cars in at the last minute too. It wasn't even full.

We both looked at my fishbowl, with the fish slowly moving around, coming up to the surface, searching for food. At that moment, I wished I was in there too, calm, enclosed, fed, safe.

'You going to give them some lunch then?'

It all felt so final. I reached for the small tub of goldfish flakes, popped the lid and sprinkled in a few more than usual.

'Who's going to look after them when I'm gone, Pauline?'

'Don't you worry about that, I'll make sure they're safe.'

I put the lid back on the fish food and zipped up the suitcase on my bed. Rose put her head around the door.

'All set?' she asked. I couldn't speak. This felt too strange. There was so much I didn't know about what my immediate future might hold. I was worried Brett might be at Aycliffe too, then nothing would change apart from the fact that I was miles away from the few people who loved me.

'Does my mother know?' I asked Rose.

'She's been told, yes.'

I wasn't expecting her to make contact personally, but she hadn't even left a message for me. Nobody in my family had.

I picked up my case and followed Pauline out of my room, turning for one last glance. I wondered how long my other bits and pieces would stay there before being broken or stolen by the other kids. But for once, I couldn't have cared less. Apart from my fish, I had all the possessions I really wanted in the suitcase. They could fight over the rest.

There was an urgency about Rose. She wanted to get going, to get me away from Farmlands before the others kicked up a fuss. A quiet exit before the end of the school day. She was waiting by the door with a woman from Durham Social Services, who was driving us there.

Gary wasn't at Farmlands that day because he was off-shift, but he told Rose to let me know that he'd come and see me as soon as he could. I put my case in the boot and gave Pauline a hug, promising to let her know how I was getting on. Then we got in – me in the back, Rose at the front and the other lady in the driver's seat. As the engine started, I wound down my window and waved at Pauline. Pulling away, I noticed she was dabbing her eyes.

The area of Newton Aycliffe had much more of a countryside feel to it than Nottingham, less built up with wider spaces. A bit posher. We approached the Young People's Centre down a tree-lined street. The only gaps in the foliage were for some staff apartments, set back on the left and right. There was a U-shaped green in the middle, then in front of that, the open units, where people could come and go more freely.

Then round the corner and just behind was the secure unit. It looked a bit space-age, almost futuristic. It seemed so modern compared to Farmlands and Willowdene. I was surprised at how clean and welcoming it looked. If you didn't know, you'd wouldn't have guessed that it was a place for vulnerable children. It was only when the three of us got out of the car and walked up to the door, that I realised just *how* secure it was.

We were met outside by the woman in charge, who seemed friendly. She had a keycard on the end of a lanyard which she used, as well as tapping in a code on a keypad, to get us through the first door. Once in, she made sure the first door was properly locked behind us. It was like we were in an entrance hall. Then she took us through the next door in the same way, which led us to the reception area. I was told to leave all my belongings there, so they could search them for anything dodgy – then I would get them back a couple of hours later.

To be honest, I liked the feel of the place. It did feel safe. It was light and airy because all the doors had toughened glass panels in, so you could see where people were – there was no chance of anyone hiding behind them. It sounds weird, but it was exciting being somewhere completely different, where I didn't know anyone. There was also the fact that I didn't think I'd be there for long, only until everything was cleared up and people realised that Brett was to blame.

The place was split into four units – Heron, Siskin, Merlin and Royston. Royston was set off to one side, away from everybody else because they had some very special cases in there. Merlin tended to be for the girls and then Heron and Siskin were for the other boys. I was on Siskin, which was a slightly more relaxed environment. There was a lounge with a television, which had a much more comfortable feel than Farmlands.

Rose was allowed to come with me when I was shown to my bedroom. One of the first things I noticed, other than the décor of the place, was that there were more staff. The ratio of adult to child seemed much better and I immediately sensed they were more engaged, bothered about what was going on, even chatting and interacting. It felt busier than Farmlands, but nicer. One kid even said 'hi' to me as we passed.

My bedroom was basic. A single bed, desk, wardrobe and drawers. Rose brushed her hand across the desk and checked her fingers for dust, noting with a smile that everything was clean.

'You could have all your *Star Trek* and East 17 posters on that wall,' she said.

'I might put the Starship one in the middle and all the others around it,' I replied.

'Good idea. And then when you get all your things back from reception, you can put your duvet cover on and everything. It'll feel nice in no time.'

I noticed there was a curtain over the small window in the door too, so it already felt more private. I knew I'd probably want to stay in my room for the first few days, just until I got more settled, but the whole atmosphere felt less oppressive than anywhere I'd been for a long time.

After about ten minutes, there was nothing more to say and Rose needed to head back. We had a bit of an awkward hug and she turned to leave.

'You'll be safe here. All these other children, they don't know about anything, about what Brett was making you do. It's a clean slate.'

I nodded and gave her a thumbs up.

'See you soon then,' I said.

I watched her head back down the corridor, then closed my door and walked over to my bed, where I sat and took in my new surroundings. I was sad that I wouldn't be able to see Gary, Rose, Avril, Pauline or Anna for a while, but if that was the price to pay to keep Brett away from me, it was worth it.

About a month later, I went to court on three consecutive days for the trial. It felt so alien because even though I'd given evidence against the paedophile in London, that was by videolink. I'd never actually been in a courtroom before with a judge and jury, people in suits and official looking men and women buzzing around. None of the people I loved were there, nobody from my family. On my side it was just me with someone from Aycliffe for support, and a solicitor. I had no idea what was happening and felt very much on my own.

The case drew a lot of local media attention. After all, a shopping centre had been burned down, causing three million pounds worth of damage. And speculation that it was likely to be two care home kids behind it added an extra layer of interest.

In court, it felt like they didn't care about the facts. They just saw two teenagers blaming each other, with no parents to answer to. Because we were both at the scene, it was almost like an open and shut case. They'd seen the CCTV footage of me in the coat buying lighter fluid at various petrol stations.

Brett told them that it was all my idea, that I started the fire. The judge looked at my previous convictions and saw I had a couple of cautions for other things. But he must have also seen Brett's case notes with earlier arson offences.

'He's lying,' I shouted. 'Tell the truth, tell them what

happened Brett. You started that fire, not me. You *made* me buy the lighter fluid so you could get high.'

Brett was acting like this was the best day of his life. He was actually smiling, excited, like the whole experience was thrilling him. Even though I knew he couldn't do anything to me while we were in court, the sight of him still frightened me. He seemed psychotic. I was particularly petrified of ending up in the same place as him again, where he would undoubtably re-assert his control.

When the conviction was read out, I burst into tears.

I was sentenced to four years for arson, remaining at Aycliffe Young People's Centre. I thought my life was over. Brett, who was seventeen now, got five years for arson in a Young Offenders Institute. It would have been 'arson with intent to endangering life' but thankfully nobody was around.

Brett cheered as he was led away.

I could barely lift my head up. It just felt so wrong. A hopeless situation where nobody in authority believed me. Again. As we left the back of the court, tears streaming down my face, flanked by a member of staff from Aycliffe, there were reporters shouting questions, jostling for answers. A press photographer pushed forward and took a picture of my face.

Gary and Rose were on shift together at Farmlands when they received news of the verdict. They quietly went to the family room, sat down and just shook their heads. Both shed tears for me privately.

'The poor kid,' Rose said.

'I feel like I've really let him down,' Gary replied.

Gary believes I was wrongly, harshly convicted. He thinks the severity of the punishment was because money was involved due to all the building repair work needed. He feels they didn't take into consideration the fact that it was *me* who called the fire service, or that I'd clearly been coerced into the situation.

They both wished they could have done more for me while I was living at Farmlands, but my conviction was a real turning point for Gary. He felt that after years in the system, trying his hardest to help so many vulnerable children, he'd achieved very little. He wanted to do more to support staff working in children's homes to ensure the right people got proper back-up, so eventually went to work full-time for UNISON.

Pauline was distraught and wanted to come and see me straight away, but we had to make do with telephone calls to start off with. Avril simply couldn't believe it and Anna was devastated, because to all intents and purposes, I was her little boy. She stuck by me and visited every two weeks until I was released.

Nobody in my family reached out.

As it turned out, other than one horrific incident on my very first night there, I think Aycliffe Young People's Centre was the making of me.

16

•

The Incident

PAULINE IS very perceptive. During our initial phone calls before the trial, she always asked me how I was filling my days, what the staff and other children were like, if I was eating properly and learning my spellings at the school there. I tried to put a positive a spin on things because it made it easier for me to believe.

But there was something I couldn't bring myself to tell Pauline about for a long time. We'd chat about all sorts for ten minutes or so, then the incident would surface in my mind, and I'd clam up. I didn't want to think about it, so kept it to myself. To say it out loud would make it real and I'd already been told by a member of staff at Aycliffe that it was pointless reporting it to the police because it wouldn't change the sentence of the perpetrator anyway.

On that very first night at the Young People's Centre, I was raped by one of the older boys. It only happened once, and it was the last sexual assault I encountered while in the care system. But it was violent and harrowing and felt like the final straw. I'm not going to go into details, but he was as brutal and degrading as the man on the dirty mattress in the industrial unit on the night of the fire.

Brett had silenced me by fear – and look where that had got me. But if this attack did anything, it filled me with justified rage. How dare this boy I didn't know, do that to me and not expect consequences? After everything I'd been through over the years I vowed, as he left me shaking, that I would not keep quiet.

After he swaggered off, I left it a few minutes then alerted the Wing Manager, telling them what had just happened. I was all over the place. They could have taken samples for evidence, looked through the internal CCTV and seen how he got into my room. I had nothing to lose, I was in the right. But though they believed me and sympathised, their advice was not to press charges. They dealt with the matter internally and the boy was moved elsewhere. I never saw him again.

That incident taken alone would be enough to psychologically damage someone for life, but because of everything that had gone before, I needed to minimise the severity in my mind, file it away in my ever-increasing mental folder of 'abuse'.

Pauline kept gently pushing during our phone calls though, she knew I was holding something back and eventually, I broke and gave her a sanitised version of events. I told her that my first night had been awful, that one of the boys had forced himself on me, but that I'd told staff and it had been dealt with. Pauline was devasted.

'Oh, my poor boy. What are they doing to you?' she cried.

'It's OK Pauline. I'm OK. He's gone now, he's not here, don't worry.' Hearing her upset made me upset. The reality, the severity of what had happened dawned on me, and I started crying too. In the end, I just said that I didn't want to think about it anymore and Pauline, true to her word, never mentioned it again for my sake.

But with that still weighing heavily on my mind, on top of the recent court case, I was struggling to cope. Whichever direction I went for help I was batted back by the very people who were meant to be on my side. To my mind, I was fair game for anyone who could find a way to get what they wanted from me. I couldn't see an end in sight, and I attempted to take my own life again.

In my bedroom, the window opened a couple of inches wide, with mesh preventing it going any further. I tied my dressing gown cord around the handle, then around my neck and dropped to the floor to try and hang myself. It was a desperate attempt, but it was all I could think of. I'd failed to slash my wrists when I was living at Farmlands, so I felt this was my only option. I needed an end to the constant churning in my head. I'd been in survival mode for so long that I didn't know what it felt like to exist without turmoil and fear.

Richie – Who Cares?

Needless to say, it didn't work. It's frustrating that I can't remember the full facts of every incident – because there were just so many. But I have a feeling a staff member found me trying to do it and raised the alarm. It was probably more of a cry for help than anything. It's not that I wanted to be dead, I just couldn't face the future as it was. There were so many hurdles in my path to a normal, happy life. I'd seen glimpses of how it could be with Pauline's family, experienced it with Anna, but now my contact with them was limited.

Something about that failed attempt gave me a new resolve though. I realised that by trying to take my own life, I was letting the abusers win and I wanted to be better than them. I wanted to free myself from their clutches once and for all and figured the best way to beat them was to end up with a decent life, being a good person. I never wanted to be forced into prostitution again. I never wanted to hide from frightening men or women. I didn't want to live in poverty or be dragged into drug abuse and I hated violence of any kind.

I began viewing Aycliffe as a bit of a Godsend. Everything I needed was in this one secure place, away from Brett, Carl, Kevin, Jake, Shane and my mother – they couldn't stop me. It was my chance to escape everything that had gone before and carve out my own path. I grasped every opportunity that came my way.

I gradually fell into a routine at the Young People's Centre, going to school Monday to Friday. All four houses – Heron, Siskin, Merlin and Royston intermingled in the large outdoor communal area first thing in the morning before going into lessons. In addition to standard classrooms, there was a home economics area, science lab, woodwork block, a gym, sports hall and swimming pool.

The curriculum was largely the same as a standard school, with a bit more emphasis on practical skills. There were a lot of children like me who missed out on learning for one reason or another, which made for plenty of disruption in lessons. Many weren't used to the discipline of sitting still and listening. For the teachers at Aycliffe, it was probably more about crowd control than meaningful preparation for GCSE's.

I enjoyed learning how to make cakes in home economics, and loved swimming because I was pretty good, having earned a couple of badges from when I was allowed to go with primary school. But the gym was my favourite place, because the feeling of accomplishment after a hard work-out was amazing. The only class I didn't like was drama, it seemed pointless.

I made a couple of casual friends there, but nobody I wanted to keep in touch with. I tried smoking for a bit, just to fit in, but I didn't like it and used to cough my guts up. After witnessing my brother Luke being forced to eat a plate of cigarette ends by my mother, I'd been put off for life.

I focused on making my room as nice as possible and used the sewing classes to make a great *Star Trek* pillow. It was quite a homophobic environment there, but I never wanted to hide that side of myself. One member of staff was always on my side though, and she fought for my right to have my calendar of choice.

At weekends, we were allowed visits from family and friends. None of my family came to see me, but I really looked forward to spending time with the positive people in my life. Gary and Rose turned up on my first birthday in there – and brought a Simpsons cake. It was really funny because on the top of it was iced the word 'DOH' – which pretty much summed up my life at the time.

I was keen to show them my bedroom with my new *Star Trek* pillow and prove that I still had the cassettes Gary had given me. I was a bit hyper to be honest, but after a few more visits, became calmer, and started to ask about their lives instead of only focusing on myself. For the first time, I wasn't looking over my shoulder waiting for someone to hurt me. It was the closest to normal I had ever experienced.

When Anna visited (usually on Sundays), we talked about anything and everything. Sometimes her housemate Mick came with her, and they'd tell me about gigs they'd played; or we'd get a board game out or have something to eat, just basic things. I still felt very protective of my relationships though, so often preferred to keep my guests in my bedroom rather than using the communal area. I just didn't want anyone else trying to muscle in.

It soon became clear to staff at Aycliffe that I wasn't posing a risk to anyone else or myself. I was kind, polite and engaging and because of this, I was gradually given more freedoms. One of those was being able to leave the unit with Anna for a few hours at a time – and that was special.

It felt completely natural being with Anna. We never ventured too far because she'd already travelled a couple of hours to get to me, but we sometimes went to the cinema or McDonalds. Occasionally we messed about in the park and had an ice cream, and she often bought me a magazine to take back with me. Prior to my move to Aycliffe, when I stayed with Anna over the weekends, I never discussed what went on at Farmlands, but as time went on in this new environment, I felt more comfortable straying into that territory with her.

Unlike at Farmlands, when I was dropped back after a few hours out, I didn't feel totally bereft and scared. Even going through security was fine because the staff made the process seem as casual and normal as possible. I wasn't there to be punished; I was there to be kept safe.

Other kids often wanted to show off their visitors, to make themselves look popular. One of those other kids turned out to be Jared – the son of my dad's new wife. I don't know what had happened for him to be in Aycliffe, but it was uncomfortable living on the same wing as him. For the most part, we avoided each other. He didn't like me because I was gay and I didn't like him because he was a spoiled brat. I don't think staff had twigged we had a family connection.

I was sitting in my bedroom, watching the coverage of Princess Diana's funeral from earlier that week. It's strange, but the mood in the unit was very quiet. Obviously, nobody knew Diana, but somehow, her death struck a chord with a lot of people.

I usually liked to keep my door closed when I could, but on this occasion, it was slightly ajar and the curtain across the window section was pulled open. For a moment, I thought I could hear my dad's voice drifting down the corridor, but then dismissed it as wishful thinking and carried on watching TV. But then I heard it again and jumped off my bed to look out of my door. There, just metres away, were Jared, Dawn and my dad walking towards Jared's room. 'Dad?' I shouted.

He turned around, looking as shocked as me.

Had he no idea I was living here? Had nobody bothered to tell him? Did he think I was still at Farmlands? I rushed over. This was so unexpected. I hadn't seen him since my last visit with Pauline almost three years before. He looked just the same – scruffy. Dawn looked like a startled animal, she clearly hadn't been expecting to see me either.

'What are you doing here?' I asked my dad.

'Oh, we've come to see Jared,' he replied.

It was a real body blow. I couldn't believe that he'd visit Dawn's son but not his own flesh and blood. Why would he do that? 'Oh,' was all I could muster initially.

To make matters worse, when people had visitors, other children weren't allowed to get involved, so I shouldn't have even been talking to him. I wasn't having any of that though.

'Er, how is everyone?' I continued, 'How's Luke and Claire, grandma and grandad? Do they know I'm here?'

'Didn't you know? Your grandma died,' he said.

What?

'When? What happened?'

'I dunno. About two years ago, I think.'

In the space of minutes, I'd unexpectedly seen my dad visiting someone else and found out my lovely grandma had died. I was dumbstruck. The last time I'd seen grandma was with Pauline.

'Why didn't anyone tell me?' I asked.

'Not sure. Maybe they thought you already knew.'

'And why have you come to see Jared and not me?' I said, my voice getting louder 'I'm your son, not him. It's me you should be visiting.'

Dawn stood in front of my father and Jared, like she was shielding them from an attack. My voice had alerted staff to the fact that something was going on and the wing manager came bustling over.

'This is *my dad*,' I shouted at the wing manager.

'Your dad?' she asked, looking from me to my dad, to Jared and Dawn.

'Yes, he's my bloody dad and he's visiting Jared.'

Jared was smirking, seeing how upset I was, knowing he'd got one over on me.

Then I lost it and lurched towards them. I was so upset and confused as to why he was here, telling me my grandma was dead like it was no big deal. Why had nobody told me before? The wing manager intervened and tried to usher me back into my room.

'At least just tell me what happened to grandma,' I pleaded.

Dad, Dawn and Jared moved along the corridor away from me and my dad didn't answer. He didn't even look back. But Jared did – throwing me a snide grin. He knew how much this was hurting and he was reveling in it.

I was heartbroken, I wished I hadn't seen dad at all.

I sat on my bed and with my head in my hands, let tears of frustration fall. I was so deflated. I'd been doing everything right – knuckling down, avoiding the kids who were trouble, getting on with staff and trying to prove I wasn't like the others. But at every single turn there seemed to be a fresh trauma to face.

About five minutes later, the wing manager came into my room and perched on the end of the mattress. I sensed she wanted to put her arm around my shoulders to soothe me, but of course, that wasn't allowed. Instead, she gently asked me what the story was, I told her how I knew Jared, about my mother's lies poisoning everyone against me, how I'd been taken to Willowdene and everything getting worse from there.

She was kind. She understood. She knew I was a victim of circumstances which had spiraled way out of control.

'Here,' she said, passing me a couple of clean tissues from her pocket.

'Thanks,' I sniveled. 'I didn't know my grandma was dead. The last time I saw her was with Pauline when I lived at Farmlands.'

'It's hard when someone you love dies,' she said, reaching for my hand.

'I just really loved her. She was so kind, and she loved me. I didn't even get chance to say goodbye and now I don't even know where she's buried or anything. Or who went to the funeral. Nobody tells me anything. It's like I'm not part of the family at all.'

She squeezed my hand and we sat there silently for a while as I caught my breath and wiped my eyes.

'Let me see what I can find out for you. I know it can't be easy.'

'Thank you,' I said 'I didn't mean to get so riled, it's just that I wasn't expecting to see my dad and then get that news. I can't get my head around it.'

'It's a lot to take in, but I promise I'll find out what I can for you.'

She got up and handed me one more tissue, then headed off, closing the door softly behind her. I can't remember being told anymore details about her death whilst I was at Aycliffe, but that's not to say they didn't let me know. My overriding memory is of the moment I found out.

Within a week, Jared was moved to another wing.

My dad never visited me.

17

•

Finding Me

IT WASN'T easy coming to terms with the death of my grandma, but the blow was softened slightly by being granted Exeat. That meant, in addition to being able to leave the facility for a few hours with Anna, I was also allowed supervised trips away from Aycliffe for other activities. I threw myself into everything.

I went canoeing, horse riding, rock climbing and abseiling. I signed up for the ski trip to Aviemore and ended up getting a two-star bronze skiing award. It was absolutely brilliant to finally be getting a taste of what life should be like, stepping out of my comfort zone, meeting new people and broadening my horizons. Never in my wildest dreams would I have imagined being able to go skiing when I was that little boy, locked in a bedroom, starved by my mother.

One of the staff members at the Young People's Centre was a big rugby union fan and supported Barnard Castle. He took me to a match, and I was hooked. Watching the game reminded me of Anna's dad and cheering for Scotland.

I knew the rules and could follow the game closely, soon adopting Barnard Castle as my new local team. After a few matches, I expressed an interest in playing.

A try-out was arranged and after practicing with them for a while, I was allowed to join. It was great, not just because it was another reason for me to be away from the unit, but because I was treated the same as the rest of the team, which was a major confidence booster. I loved the structure and discipline, and always felt on a real high after running around the pitch for eighty minutes.

On 26th January 1999 I was told I'd be able to leave Aycliffe earlier than expected. I was sixteen. It came with conditions and I had a few months to get used to the idea before packing up all my belongings and stepping out to freedom. I was so happy that staff and officials knew I was a good person. To me, that was just as important as being able to walk out of there. They saw how determined I was, against all the odds, to do the right thing and better myself. I wondered if it was my quick reaction to an horrific incident shortly before that announcement which had sealed the deal.

There were two boys in Aycliffe who were nasty to say the least. One of them was there for murdering an eighty-four-year-old woman and was due to go to a Young Offenders' Institute as soon as he hit sixteen. The other was his sidekick. I was in the main area of the building, sat at one of the tables near the kitchen, talking to one of the older workers there, Jan. The recreation room was just in front of us.

Suddenly, there was a commotion as the two lads ran into the recreation room and set upon a member of staff who held keys to the place. It all happened so quickly. They just seemed to pounce, throwing snooker balls at his head and beating him with the cues. The other kids at Aycliffe heard what was happening and started egging the lads on, but Jan and I didn't know what to do. It was so frightening – they were like animals.

Jan was shouting and screaming for them to stop, and tried to intervene, but then they turned on her and began battering her with the cues.

They were feral.

'I've got them,' one of the lads yelled, detaching a bunch of keys from the male workers belt, 'let's go'.

They were completely crazed, jumping around, laughing and cheering – and then they were gone. They ran off, opening and closing doors with the stolen keys, steps away from freedom, leaving a trail of devastation behind them.

When the other kids saw the reality of what had happened, what they had encouraged and taken part in, they scarpered. Jan just about managed to raise the alarm and I went over to the male staff member who was laid on the floor. Seeing blood oozing from his head, I rushed straight to the kitchen and made a cold compress from a tea-towel, then dashed back and pressed it to the wound. He must have been in agony.

I told him to stay still and that the alarm had been raised. Then I ran back to the kitchen to make another compress for Jan. I couldn't believe what a vicious attack it had been. It was absolutely horrible to witness. When more staff arrived, they ordered the remaining children to stay in their rooms, but I was allowed to help, and was asked for my version of events.

While all this was happening, the two boys not only made it out of the building but got into a car with keys that had also been attached to the bunch. They sped off, tyres screeching, and hurtled along the main road to get out of Newton Aycliffe as fast as they could. They didn't make it very far.

The next day, we were all told the car had hit a tree, killing one of them and leaving the other seriously injured.

With a date set for release, my thoughts were turning to the future. It was only a few weeks until I'd be on my own. After all this time hoping and dreaming of being free from the care system, it suddenly seemed quite daunting, because like most sixteen-year-olds, I had no idea what I wanted to do. The only thing I *did* know was that I didn't want to turn out like my peers. The positive influences of Pauline, Gary, Rose, Avril and Anna had seeped into my consciousness, and I believed that somehow, I could make a good life for myself.

I also had this weird thing in my head, where I was always wishing I'd stay alive long enough to make it to the age of twenty-two, when I'd have a house, car and a good partner. It's sad that I could only imagine getting to that young age, but I honestly used to think: *Don't take me now, let me get to there. Let me have that. Let me enjoy it and if you want to kill me, kill me after that.* It was something to aspire to amidst the terror.

I don't know why twenty-two was the imaginary cut-off point. I knew that at sixteen, I'd be free, but I kept thinking: *Come on, you can get through this. Get this done and get to that stage.* I wanted to survive and make sense of the awful times to experience what it would be like to have a happier existence.

In the run up to leaving Aycliffe Young People's Centre, I had various discussions with social workers about my hopes. It all seemed so vague and unachievable though. There were a number of jobs I was interested in doing – I loved outdoor pursuits and wondered if I could teach those skills to others. I fancied training to be a scuba diver, but what career could you have with that? Most of what I wanted to do involved helping other people. Becoming a paramedic really appealed to me or working for the police. But essentially, the priority for staff at Aycliffe was to get me earning so I could support myself as soon as possible.

There was also the issue of where I was going to live. Not just in terms of a roof over my head – but location too. Nottinghamshire County Council were still meant to be responsible for me because that's where I was taken into care. But Aycliffe was under the umbrella of Durham County Council, so I had a foot in both camps. I was encouraged to live near either friends or family, so a support network was close to hand.

Nottingham wasn't really an option. I felt that I'd come a long way to escape the clutches of Brett and his horrendous cycle of abuse and was desperate to avoid any chance of being dragged back into the abyss. I knew of people who had moved to halfway houses in Nottingham and it hadn't ended well for them. Those places were riddled with drug users and young adults who couldn't break free from sexual exploitation. They were basically just holding pens for the prison system and utterly depressing.

The problem was that I didn't know anybody in the Durham region either and I didn't want to be cast adrift. Anna suggested that it would be a good idea to live near Burnley, so I could be near to her should I need anything. After a lot of too-ing and fro-ing with councils, they found me a bedsit in shared social-services-run house there with one other person in it. I moved in on 22nd March 1999.

Richie – Who Cares?

The night before was strange. I had everything packed way before I needed to, keen to get the wheels in motion. I'd accumulated a lot more stuff than at Farmlands or Willowdene, so my suitcase was stuffed. I double checked I'd received everything back from laundry, including my bedding and favourite Craghoppers fleece from outdoor pursuits club. In my smaller rucksack I had my radio alarm clock, a couple of cars which I knew I was too old for, and my Walkman with tapes from Gary.

My room looked bare as I laid on my bed for a final sleep in the Young People's Centre. I stared at the tiny marks on the walls where blue tack had held up my posters. There was a slightly brighter, cleaner square of paint where my much-loved boys calendar had prevented the sunshine fading that patch. My shelves were empty without schoolbooks, and I remembered the first time I walked in, with Rose dragging her hand along the top to check for dust.

After a rocky start I'd made the most of my time there and felt proud of what I'd learned. My path to Aycliffe had been horrendous, but the place saved me from a lot worse. I wondered where my brother Luke was. Did he go to a halfway house in Nottingham? And what about Claire? I hoped she was with a caring foster family at least. I suspected my mother had washed her hands of the lot of us. I decided I would try to find out once I was settled.

I was up, dressed and ready first thing in the morning, waiting for a member of staff to drive me to Burnley. After saying my goodbyes to a handful of people, I went to the office for my final instructions, where I was given some loose advice about looking after myself and handed an envelope with five hundred pounds inside for living costs. Part of me felt sad to be leaving, but I was as ready as I was ever going to be to face the outside world.

I dumped my bags in the boot and made my way to the front passenger seat. After buckling myself in, I turned to look at the building for one last time then faced straight ahead as we drove away, back up the tree-lined road with spring daffodils blowing in the wind. No looking back, it was time to move on.

The journey from Newton Aycliffe took about two hours, and

other than a bit of Simon Mayo on Radio 1 in the background, we were mainly silent. As we approached the outskirts of Burnley, it felt good to see a few familiar shops and buildings from when I spent weekends with Anna. When we eventually pulled up outside my accommodation, my heart sank though. I didn't really know what I was expecting, but this place didn't look inviting.

'Looks like we're here,' said the social worker.

'Yes. Looks like it,' I replied.

I could tell his initial thoughts were the same as mine, but he tried to keep things upbeat.

'It's probably better inside, and once you get all your stuff unpacked, it'll feel more homely.'

Homely? *Right.*

We grabbed a bag each, found where the key had been hidden for us and went in. As soon as we stepped through, the guy who lived on the ground floor appeared at his door. He nodded at us and said my room was at the top, then went back inside. The social worker turned to me.

'Okay, well, it looks like you know where you're going from here.'

'Yep.'

'You've got everything you need?'

'I think so.'

'Right, well, I'd better be getting back then. You get yourself settled in and good luck with everything,' he said, turning to leave.

'Thanks,' I replied.

And with that, he was off. And I was left there with my bags, feeling way out of my comfort zone, wondering what on earth I was going to do now. *Just get to twenty-two,* I thought, as I dragged my bags up the dirty stairwell.

The place was damp, run-down and dark with a very basic kitchen and bathroom. The guy downstairs had the run of his bedroom and the first floor, and I had my room in the loft and whatever was left. Both places were locked. It was nothing like the clean, bright Young People's Centre, full of things going on. It was freezing cold because they were stingy with the gas and electric meters and being in the attic with no insulation didn't help. It was grim. Not even my favourite calendar could brighten it up.

I was under prepared for life in general. Both Durham and Nottinghamshire County Councils had taken the fact that I'd chosen to live in Burnley as my decision to leave their care systems entirely. I wasn't anybody's specific responsibility and hadn't been given the name of anyone for a point of contact, should I need any extra help.

There was no advice about how to budget and even though I'd spent a lot of time in home economics at Aycliffe, we hadn't been taught how to shop for necessities. I didn't even know how to do my own washing because none of the children had been allowed in the laundry room in case they misused the toxic products.

I slung my bag on the bed, walked over to the grimy attic window and cracked it open to peer out on the main road below. That promising spring day had turned cold and wet. Cars with slapping windscreen wipers drove past, a couple of hooded teenagers sucked on soggy cigarettes in the betting shop doorway. I looked back inside at my grey ceiling with a bare lightbulb and felt a bit hopeless.

I scrambled in my bag for my Walkman and selected one of the tapes Gary had given me by a band called Garbage. I put my headphones on, kicked my bag down to the floor and laid on top of the bed, trainers still on, and played 'When I Grow Up'. The chorus seemed to say it all: *When I grow up, I'll be stable. When I grow up, I'll turn the tables.*

18

•

Sense of Purpose

I DIDN'T SLEEP brilliantly that night. There was too much spinning around my head.

Yes, I was out of the care system, but I had a long way to go before reaching my dream of house, car, partner, life. I got up, took a shower under a dribble of tepid water above a bath with disintegrating grout and made a mental plan; get breakfast, find a job, buy a cheap mobile phone, ring Anna. I wouldn't say I was one hundred percent optimistic, but I was determined to make the most of this situation. Everybody had to start somewhere.

I managed three of the things on my list – a bacon sandwich, a mobile and ringing Anna.

After spending a soul-destroying couple of hours at the job centre with no luck, I walked around town to see if any shops or cafes needed part time staff. They didn't. I picked up some Super Noodles and jelly pots from the market and headed back, deflated.

I was idly wondering what the other guy in the bedsit was like – what had brought him to this place and if he had a job. I doubted I'd want to be best mates with him, but if I had to live here, I thought at least we should get along. It turned out he was a thief. While I'd been out, he'd broken into my room, stolen a load of my stuff and scarpered.

I was absolutely devastated. What hurt the most was that he took my music and Craghoppers fleece. What he didn't take, he'd left strewn around on the floor. I hadn't even properly unpacked, yet the draws had been yanked open and left hanging, two wire coat-hangers dangled in the wardrobe and my toothpaste had been swiped from my sink.

I'd barely managed twenty-four hours out of care and I was already on my knees again.

I desperately needed to speak to Anna, so plugged in my new phone to charge and waited for it to slowly come to life. I knew her number off by heart, having rung so many times from Farmlands and Aycliffe, but this wasn't the phone call I'd been hoping to make. I'd imagined telling her that I was settled in, with a job lined up and my room all sorted. I wanted Anna to feel proud of me, but instead I just had another disaster story for her. As it rang, I could feel myself getting more and more emotional, forcing back the tears and trying to keep my breathing steady.

'Hello,' Anna answered.

'It's all gone wrong,' I blurted out.

'What's happened?'

I told her everything and she sounded as upset as me.

'Pack whatever's left, and we'll get you somewhere else. It's not safe for you to stay there.'

Just one phone call was all it took for me to feel better. Anna was in control, an adult and somebody who cared enough to get me out of there asap. It didn't take long to gather everything together, but I made sure to leave it as I found it, with the drawers closed, bed stripped and blind down. I wasn't sorry to be seeing the back of the place, but I was upset that my first taste of freedom had ended so badly, so quickly.

I didn't want to hang around in case the other guy came back. For all I knew, he could have been dangerous and the last thing I wanted was another altercation. I agreed to meet Anna in a café just around the corner and by teatime, she'd arrived and driven me back to her place. It felt strange being back in Anna's house after all this time. I hadn't been there since before the fire.

We ate, then put plan 'B' into action. Anna found me a privately owned bedsit on Padiham road in Burnley, paid the bond and my first month's rent. It was an old Victorian end terrace, and my room was on the side of the building. I could see The Tim Bobbin pub across the road and a row of shops. I couldn't have been more relieved or grateful to her in that moment. It wasn't flash, but it was warm, dry and safe. It was my own space away from drama and a starting point for better things to come.

Not only did Anna come to the rescue with accommodation, but her friend Heather stepped in to find me a job. Heather worked at the Town & Country Club in Leeds – a nightclub and music venue in the city centre. I think she was part of the management team and got me a position working in the burger bar downstairs, where I began as a pot washer and ended up serving food. It was a whole new world.

I was kind of giddy at first because I didn't really know how to handle myself in public very well. Customers at The Town & Country Club were mainly aged between eighteen to mid-twenties, a young crowd intent on having fun. Some were students, some had jobs, but they were all here for a good time. This was new territory for me, so Heather really took me under her wing and showed me the ropes.

I loved that nobody who came to the club had any idea about my previous life. I could be who I wanted to be without question. I could chat away, flirt, and at the end of my shift, hit the dancefloor with everybody else. It was absolutely great.

The best night of all was when the club hosted Mr Gay UK 1999. My eyes were on stalks. Here I was, a gay sixteen-year-old boy, surrounded by some of the most handsome men in the UK. There were oiled up muscle-bound blokes on the stage, there were guys grinding on the dancefloor and every possible shape, size and leaning asking me for burgers. It was heaven.

The money was crap, but I didn't mind. By the time I'd commuted to Leeds from Burnley and back for my shifts there was little left to spare, but topped up by housing benefit, I was scraping by and began to feel genuinely optimistic about my future. I just wanted to enjoy my freedom for a while before looking for something more sustainable. The most important thing for me at that time was having the freedom to make my own choices.

Richie – Who Cares?

I was keen to play rugby again and, as it happened, a colleague of Anna's mums' was a coach for Burnley RUFC. I had a trial and began training with the team, eventually becoming a winger because I was so fast. The guys on the team knew I was gay but couldn't have cared less. It was so liberating. They were typical rugby lads, taking the piss out of me, but I enjoyed the banter and gave as good as I got.

It was great socially too and one night after winning a match, I drank way too much John Smiths and ate far too many portions of pie and peas, all of which I threw up in the sink in my bedsit when I got back. But as my head spun, I couldn't have felt any happier.

There was still something niggling me though. The only qualification I gained at Aycliffe Young People's Centre was an NVQ in woodwork. I'd left in the March and my GCSE's were in June, but no provision had been made for me to sit them elsewhere. In September, I enrolled at Burnley College. I used my real name for the application but when I started, asked everyone from then on to call me Richie – a shortened version of my middle name. I wanted nothing more to do with the name my mother had given me.

Initially, I enjoyed college and made a handful of friends. It felt good to be learning and for the next few months my days and nights were filled with work, college and rugby, giving me a real sense of purpose heading towards Year 2000.

The night of the millennium was funny. I was seventeen and had been invited to a house party by one of the lads at college. His parents were out, so about twenty of us all piled over with bottles of Hooch and Watermelon Bacardi Breezers. We got absolutely ruined, but at about eleven o'clock his parents arrived back unexpectedly early and kicked everyone out. We weren't deterred though, we just took our Hooch and wandered the streets, waiting for the Y2K fireworks.

We were all talking about the millennium bug and wondering if aeroplanes would fall from the sky or if trains would de-rail, like all the conspiracists were saying. We thought it would be great if

ATMs started spitting out money and fantasised about what we'd spend it on. I don't remember making any specific New Year resolutions, but I did secretly thank my lucky stars that I was right there, with those people, living independently in Burnley.

I gave a drunken thought to where my family might be celebrating and assumed my mother would be high somewhere with a new boyfriend. Luke would have been nearly nineteen at that point and Claire about fifteen. I hoped they were safe and prayed that my stepdad was as far away from my sister as possible.

Some of the group had split off to find another party, but a bunch of us stuck around outside to see in the New Year. We could hear the countdown through someone's lounge window and joined in outside.

5-4-3-2-1... Welcome to the Millennium!

We jumped around and clinked bottles, not feeling the cold one bit. When we were out of alcohol, we all said our goodbyes and went on our ways – some of them linking arms, wondering if it might be their lucky night. But I just weaved my way back to my bedsit, let myself in and fell asleep on the chair, happy to be alive.

Some friends you keep for life and others, you realise, aren't really your bag. As I got to know people at college a bit more, conversations naturally turned to families and upbringings. I didn't tell them everything (because honestly, where do you start with something like that?) but they knew I'd spent most of my childhood in care, was gay and didn't have contact with my immediate family.

I suspect they didn't know how to react to that kind of information as most of them probably hadn't come from abusive backgrounds. I felt like I was gradually being filtered out from the main group and left at the bottom of the pile with the outcast kids. The kids with physical or learning disabilities. It was a harsh lesson, but I tried not to let it phase me and instead, turned my attention to finding a better social life. I stumbled across a gay bar in Burnley.

Because I'd been working at The Town & Country Club in Leeds for a while now, I was used to seeing people having fun, interacting and dancing – but for the most part, I'd been a member of staff there. At the gay bar, I was simply a single guy looking to let loose, drink, and meet new people on my terms. I spent a lot of time dancing to Steps and belting out 'Tragedy' on the karaoke machine. It was a blast.

I also started looking for another job, closer to where I lived. I disliked the fact that I was on any kind of benefits and wanted to support myself fully as soon as I could. JJB Sports in Burnley were hiring and to my surprise, I got a role as a sales assistant. Initially, I kept working in Leeds too, so life was pretty full, and I was pleased with the path I was on.

I wanted to let Gary and Pauline know how I was doing, so rang Gary and he came to see me in Burnley. Then not long after, I visited Pauline at her house in Nottingham.

Gary had real concerns for me leaving Aycliffe. He'd seen so many other children wind up in a life of crime, poverty or abuse because it was all they'd grown up with, but he was always rooting for me.

'Blimey, you've grown,' was the first thing he said to me when I opened the door to my bedsit.

I was beaming. It was so good to see him face to face again, in a setting that was out of the care system. There was no reason for him to be here other than out of choice and that felt great. It really cemented what I'd always hoped would be a long-lasting friendship. He seemed impressed that I'd found work and was supporting myself, and said he felt immensely proud of how far I'd come.

Over lunch in a café in Burnley, Gary asked a lot of questions about how I was feeling, what I thought I might do next and if I was happy. I wanted to know what he was up to having left Farmlands, and who he kept in touch with. He was still acting like a concerned dad, and I loved that. I knew I'd always be able to turn to him for advice in the future.

When I arrived at Pauline's house a couple of weeks later, she opened the door and just hugged me. She wouldn't let me go for ages and got very emotional.

'Look at you. You're all grown,' she said, wiping tears from her eyes.

'I got tall,' I said, grinning. 'It must have been all the chicken you cooked for me.' Her children were there too and so we spent a lot of time catching up, as Pauline made my favourite meal again. God, it tasted good.

Pauline was of a similar mindset to Gary – she was only too aware of the potential pitfalls for a child who'd endured such a chaotic start in life, so my visit was a big moment for her too. She could tell that I wanted to do something useful with my future and was distancing myself from those horrendous early years.

It was so lovely to be welcomed back into her home, but even lovelier to know that when it was time to go, I wasn't being driven back to Farmlands. I didn't get that horrible feeling of dread in my tummy as I left because this time, I was making my own way back to my own place, where I had nothing to fear and nobody telling me what I could and couldn't do.

Just like with Gary, when we finally said our goodbyes, I knew Pauline would continue to be a positive person in my life, someone who had my back, no matter what. And few years later, just like in Aycliffe when she sensed there was something amiss, Pauline pulled me to one side and asked me if everything was alright.

I'd been in Burnley for about twelve months when I met Roger at the gay bar. I was seventeen and he was mid-fifties. He was a lorry driver living in Keighley with his parents and spent a lot of time cruising around gay bars in Manchester, Liverpool and Burnley – wherever his working route took him.

He was friendly at first, buying me a few drinks, paying for the odd thing, just behaving like a nice bloke who had a bit more money than me. It didn't seem odd because he knew I wasn't earning much. We even had a bit of a laugh to start off with.

Then gradually, the coercion came along. It wasn't blatant, more implied, like he'd just bought me a load of drinks, was a nice guy and so when he started making moves, I kind of felt obliged. I didn't want to offend him. It didn't feel like it did when I was at the children's homes being pimped out because that was all very upfront – I was handed cash by the punters and knew what was expected of me. Roger made me feel like we were friends, and this was only an extension of our friendship.

Richie – Who Cares?

I was just making ends meet in Burnley and wanted to spread my wings a bit, so when the Manager at JJB Sports suggested a transfer to another of their outlets, in Keighley, I thought 'why not?' It was only twenty miles away and would be a change of scenery. Roger saw this as his golden opportunity to pounce. He offered to put me up in a flat just off Skipton Road, five minutes' walk from my new place of work. It sounded too good to be true. It was.

The flat wasn't anything fancy but was bigger and nicer than my place in Burnley. It had two bedrooms, a separate kitchen, bathroom and lounge area. He said I didn't need to worry too much about rent and I assumed he'd be taking the second bedroom. It soon became apparent that he wanted rent in kind. Sexual favours for a roof over my head, and I realised I'd been duped.

Anna says I went off-radar when I left Burnley. I stopped working at the Town & Country Club in Leeds and I think I felt ashamed of the situation I'd got myself into with Roger. I knew Anna would see it for what it was and I couldn't face her disappointment. I felt the same about seeing Gary and Pauline too. Until I could find a way out of this mess, I didn't want to lie by pretending everything was alright.

On top of that, Roger was very controlling and made no secret of the fact that he didn't want me keeping in touch with these other people in my life. It was a standard coercion technique, cutting the victim off from their friends.

In just less than a year since leaving Aycliffe I'd fallen into the clutches of another abuser. On the surface, things looked normal. Roger even introduced me to his parents as his 'mate'. His mum and dad were of the generation and small mindset that even if they had an inkling about what was going on, they didn't say anything. It was year 2000, the year when the legal age for sex between two males had only just been reduced from eighteen years to sixteen years.

It was in no way, shape or form any kind of relationship with Roger. He made it clear that he was still doing his own thing around the gay bars in Lancashire and even though he tried to keep a tight grip on me, I'd met a guy called Pete while Roger was 'working away'.

I felt like I needed to keep Pete low profile, not wanting any repercussions from Roger because I worried that if he found out, he'd throw me out of the flat and I'd be homeless. I didn't have enough money saved to move out.

Pete was lovely but it wasn't meant to be and we lasted about three months. There were no hard feelings, no dramas, we just went our separate ways. But through Pete, in a roundabout way, I became friends with one of his pals – Richard – after a night out with both of them in Manchester.

While the three of us were drinking, Roger turned up at the same bar, allegedly by coincidence. But because I was trying to keep Pete quiet from Roger, Richard acted as a decoy until me and Pete could disappear. It all sounds very complicated, but basically, that scenario alerted Richard to the fact that I was in a situation with Roger that I didn't want to be in. And with Richard being a fair bit older than me, he was also a fair bit wiser.

Shortly after Pete and I split up, I was transferred again by JJB Sports – this time to Bradford. I'd probably been there a couple of months when I was on the shop floor, straightening some rows of trainers, when in walked Richard. I hadn't noticed him, but he just walked over to me.

'Excuse me, but I think I know you,' he said.

I looked up and for the life of me, couldn't place him. I must have looked confused because he then went on to explain that he was a friend of Pete's and we'd met in Manchester.

'Ah, yes. Hiya,' I said.

Richard lived near Bradford and had come into town to get a few bits for his holiday, so I showed him where everything was, and we just got talking. There was something about him that I really warmed to. It was good to see a friendly face and by the time he'd made his purchases, we'd arranged to meet for a burger at lunchtime.

He told me he was a music teacher and was looking forward to relaxing over the summer. He updated me on how Pete was and asked me if I was still living in Keighley with Roger. For some reason, I felt like I could trust Richard and ended up giving him a potted version of my life story. It was a risk, because I hadn't opened up that much to anyone before. He could have easily decided to run like hell. But he didn't.

Maybe his teaching experiences gave him that extra bit of empathy because he recognised that if I'd been given the right opportunities, I'd be in a very different place. We kept in touch and then after his holiday, Richard said he wanted to help me on the road to something better, away from Roger. We met up again and I bought a *Telegraph & Argus* newspaper where we searched for another bedsit. He thought it was important for me to be able to establish my own roots.

We spotted a nice place in Kirkgate, Shipley, opposite St Paul's Parish church and not too far away from Asda. Out of the goodness of his heart, Richard paid my deposit, the first two months' rent, and then helped me move in. Never once, in all the time I've known Richard, has he asked for anything in return. He's a genuinely kind and thoughtful person who acted altruistically when I was down on my luck and I'll always be grateful for that.

I didn't tell Roger I was leaving. I waited for him to be working away, packed my stuff and went. I didn't even leave him a note and when he rang my mobile, I ignored it.

I felt settled quite soon after the move. The area was nicer and I was employed, so didn't need to start from scratch. I even treated myself to a pet gerbil, which I let run around the flat when I was in. I enjoyed being able to care for something and call it my own.

It was reassuring to know that Richard lived less than ten miles away, but he always kept a certain distance – like he was there in the background if I ever needed anything, he just let me live my life. The only other thing he did do, was introduce me to a few bars in Bradford, where he knew there were men more my age.

The Sun wasn't exactly the poshest place in town, but the atmosphere was brilliant. They had a lot of entertainment on – drag acts and that kind of thing, and there was always someone to talk to if I didn't go with Richard.

Because I was more settled, I felt comfortable enough to look for a better job and ended up working at Asda in Shipley. I went all the way through to management with them – from sales-based ordering, looking after the tills, nightshift work. Then I helped them change over to Walmart systems in five different stores. I also took on another job at a nightclub in Shipley, so not only was I earning a reasonable wage, but my social life was expanding too.

I was supporting myself financially now and didn't need any help from social services at all. My confidence was growing and my thoughts began turning to family again. I was curious to know what my parents were up to. I didn't know where my mum was living, but my dad was still in Nottingham, so I bit the bullet and went to visit him. More than anything, I felt a desire to prove to him that despite everything, I had made it out of the care system and was living a normal life.

19

•

Family Ties

MY DAD wasn't expecting me and I wasn't anticipating the grim reception I received.

When I knocked on the door, it was answered by Jared, who had been at Aycliffe Young People's Centre at the same time as me. I hadn't seen him since that incident, but this time, he wasn't smirking. 'What are you doing here?' he barked 'You've got no right to turn up now.'

'My dad lives here, so I can come whenever I want,' I said.

'Dale wasn't your brother, he was mine,' he shouted.

'I haven't come to see Dale, I've come to see my dad'

'Dale's dead.'

'What?'

'You heard.' I couldn't believe it. What was going on?

I'd turned up only a day after they'd received news that Dale had been found dead in his flat, slumped in a chair after a suspected heroin overdose.

Jared was distraught, pacing around the kitchen, trying to get his head around the situation and glaring at me, as if it was all my fault. 'Where's my dad?' I asked.

Dad came through from the lounge. It was true, he said. They were not long back from having identified Dale's body, and Dawn was inconsolable.

'She's a right mess,' he said, 'She doesn't know what to do and is blaming herself.'

I'd walked into a nightmare. Dad told me that they had requested for Dale's body to be brought to the house before the funeral, and it was due to arrive two days later. It was a very quick turnaround, but I think Dawn is Catholic and she wanted an open casket in the kitchen for friends and family to pay their respects.

It felt wrong to leave after hearing this news. I loved Dale. He was always kind to me and treated me like a little brother. I couldn't believe he was dead. In the end, I stayed until the funeral, which Jared wasn't happy about – but I'd coped with worse than bad attitudes in my life, so wasn't deterred. And even though I couldn't stand Jared, I did have a modicum of sympathy for him and understood his pain.

It was awful seeing Dale's body in the casket. His stillness shocked me. He was laid there, eyes closed, looking fast asleep, and I really struggled to keep it together in front of Dawn, dad and Jared. They didn't understand that even though I hadn't spent much time with Dale, he'd been nice to me, and for a child in the care system, any scrap of genuine affection is hard to come by. I really did feel like I'd had a connection with him.

The rest of the time at my dad's house went by in a blur. Everything felt morbid and oppressive, with the shock of Dale's death leaving everyone numb. The time wasn't right for a heart to heart about my own life, to ask my dad why he hadn't taken me out of the children's home when I was younger. I would have to park that discussion for a later date. Or maybe I'd never know. After the funeral and wake, I left with more questions than answers.

When I got back to my flat in Shipley, I felt really low. It's not that I'd been expecting a joyful reunion with my father, but my hopes of building a relationship for the future were dashed for now. I rang Richard and filled him in. He listened sympathetically and after our conversation, I felt a lot better. I had to understand that I couldn't control everything, and that it was natural to feel so empty after the death of a loved one. It was good to be able to share how I was feeling.

I was determined not to let that terrible news bring me down, though, and threw all my energy into work and socialising. I began burning the candle at both ends, not letting myself stop long enough to think about anything and as Christmas approached, I started feeling under the weather. A bit of a cold developed into a hacking cough, aches all over and utter exhaustion.

I ended up bed-bound for almost a week. Christmas Day came and went without fanfare, but I was too tired to care. I was cheered by visits from Richard with food, drinks and paracetamol and I filled the rest of my time sleeping and watching *Star Trek* DVDs. It was the beginning of a condition which reared its head again a few years later and left me needing a flu jab every winter and Covid boosters whenever possible.

I'm not the sort of person who enjoys doing nothing. If I can't do anything physical, then my mind starts racing, so all that time in bed forced me to think. I decided that just because the visit with dad hadn't gone as planned, all wasn't lost. I felt hopeful that now I was an adult, we might eventually be able to keep in touch on some level, once things had calmed down. I hadn't had chance to ask him anything about my mother – not least where she was living now, so decided to get in touch with her brother, Geoff, to see if he knew.

I wanted to see my mother face to face, as a grown up, to ask her why she lied about what happened to my sister, Claire. I wanted her to know the consequences of her actions, and for her to be sorry.

I didn't hold much hope of uncle Geoff knowing where she was or what she was doing. He said he'd look into it for me, and I didn't push it. I thought I might as well get on with my life and if I reached a point where I became desperate to see her, I could nudge him again or try another route. I was eighteen now and it was 2001 – time to move on.

Once I'd got myself well again, Richard suggested a night out to cheer me up, and we headed to The Sun. Up until this point, I hadn't had what you'd call a proper boyfriend. Pete had lasted a few months and I'd had a handful of liaisons with other men, but nothing noteworthy. That night at The Sun though, I got chatting to a guy called Phil.

After a few more drinks and a bit of dancing, I gave him my telephone number and hoped he'd ring. He left it a couple of days to be cool, then got in touch, and that was the beginning of a highly intense relationship which moved at break-neck speed. I thought I was in love. Phil was handsome, fun and had his own flat in Harrogate, so it didn't take much for him to persuade me to leave my Shipley bedsit and move in with him.

We had a great time, working hard during the day and enjoying the nightlife of Harrogate. He introduced me to a new set of people and after a while, I quit my job at the supermarket and began accepting work from the employment agency where Phil worked. The variety was good – anything from driving for an alarm fitting firm to answering phones in a call centre. Whichever job I did, I learned something new. I was like a sponge, soaking up all the experiences, always keen to better myself.

The one job I didn't enjoy though was at a kennels and cattery. I hated the fact that the animals were cooped up for most of the day. It reminded me of being a prisoner in my bedroom. There were about seventy dog cages in one area and about sixty cat pens right next door. If one cat made a noise, the dogs would go crazy, barking and carrying on, which in turn would frighten the cats – it was a constant viscous circle and I wanted something better for them. I couldn't imagine Anna's dog, Nell, ever liking it there. But even though that job made me sad, it planted a seed in my head for a business in the future.

I was earning a wage through the employment agency, but it wasn't satisfying on a personal level. I still had a desire to help others in some way, so began looking into the possibility of joining St John Ambulance. I saw it as a chance to learn new skills and maybe use it as a springboard into working for the NHS.

My interview was daunting because I knew I'd have to be honest about my past. I explained why I had ended up at Newton Aycliffe through no fault of my own and that, having been on the receiving end of ambulance care when I was very young, had always wanted to give something back. They believed that I'd shown great strength and integrity just to get where I was and accepted me for training.

I was 'buddied up' with another person from St John

ambulance for my first year – this was both to help me, and for them to be satisfied that I wasn't a risk and was fully capable of everything that was required for the job. I loved the focus it gave me and the team were great. After I learned the basics, I was able to start helping with first aid and gradually progressed to covering events, then managing the first aid units.

One of my most memorable moments was an event at Harewood House in Leeds, when a pregnant woman started having early contractions. Another team member and I had to get her from one end of the site to the entrance in a carry chair – and she was far from light. Keeping someone calm when you're sweating buckets yourself isn't the easiest task, but we got her to the waiting ambulance and off she went to have a baby. Moments like that for a volunteer are special. It made me very happy to know I'd done my bit to help keep her and her unborn baby safe.

Then one Sunday, I had a call from my uncle Geoff about my mother. He said he didn't know exactly where she was, but thought she worked at The Pleasure Beach in Blackpool. That was enough of a lead for me.

The following day I packed a small bag and caught the train to Blackpool, planning to visit all the ticket places and food venues until I came across her. It was a lot easier than I thought.

It was 10th September 2001. My mother hadn't spoken to me since I was eight years old, and my hope was that she'd have an explanation about her treatment of me growing up. Or an apology. I felt I needed to salvage something, anything, some sort of understanding because despite all the horror, I still wanted to feel part of a family.

The main drag in Blackpool was busy, but not as hectic as in the summer holidays. By now, most children were back at school so there was a mixture of an older crowd and parents with babies or toddlers. It was just warm enough for a T-shirt and hoody, and as I walked along the seafront, sweet smells of candy floss mingled with the aroma of vinegary fish and chips, taking me right back to the holiday with grandma and grandad.

I could hear distant screams of laughter from rollercoaster

riders, loud music pumping from 2-4-1 happy hour bars and the clunk-ping of coin machines in the arcades. Crashing waves were drowned out by the tacky din as I walked towards the main ticket office of the Pleasure Beach.

'Excuse me, does someone called Catherine works here?'

'Yeah, she's over by The Big One.'

It was as simple as that.

The Big One is the main rollercoaster at the Pleasure Beach, less than two minutes' walk from where I was stood. She was so close. I took a deep breath and before I had chance to change my mind, headed over and joined the queue. A strange excitement was building inside me. I thought this could be the moment I give her a second chance. I wanted to get a better look at her, but didn't want her to see me coming, so I kept out of sight behind the family in front. Finally, it was my turn. She looked up.

'Bloody hell,' she said.

Her face was a picture of pure shock. She actually smiled, but then looked immediately flustered.

'Hello,' I said.

She was so fat. She looked pale and unhealthy, and I could see a walking stick next to her chair.

'I'll have to talk to you later, there's people behind you in the queue,' she said.

I gave her my mobile number and she said she'd call me when she finished her shift.

I spent the next couple of hours in the gay bars in Blackpool. Seedy doesn't even cover it but it passed the time. I wasn't convinced she'd bother ringing, but she must have known there was no point in hiding. It was strange, I began feeling like I was ready to forgive her but as time ticked on without a phone call, my mind shifted to snippets of the past when she'd been so mean, frightening and cold. I couldn't do it. I needed to get out of there.

I stood up to leave, then my phone beeped with a message.

I've finished work. Meet me at the back of the fairground.

I picked up my bag and headed straight over. She looked smaller than I remembered. Her face seemed to be questioning why

Richie – Who Cares?

I was here but I didn't detect any sense of guilt or shame. She invited me to stay at her house for the night and I accepted.

I wanted her to see I was doing well in life, that despite the horror she subjected me to, I was happy and successful. We boarded the bus together and I paid. She didn't say thank you. We sat side by side and watched the final preparations for the famous Blackpool Illuminations as the bus headed away from the central strip. I tried to recall the last time I'd been on a bus with my mother, but the only journeys which came to mind were of me alone, heading back to Willowdene or Farmlands after nights of sexual abuse.

'We'll get off here' she said, standing up.

I followed her off the bus and along the pavement to a scruffy two bedroomed terraced house, where she lived with a man called Bernard. The front patch of lawn was overgrown and unkempt, the paint on the door was peeling off around the edges and weeds were taking over the cracks in the steps. Inside was no better. It had an aura of being unloved. I knew how it felt.

It was strange seeing her in the kitchen. I looked at the layout and wondered if she kept a jar of chilli powder hidden at the back of one of the cupboards. Was her freezer locked? Did she keep one of the bedrooms like a prison? I knew I was a grown man at nineteen years old, but those feelings of being a scared little boy resurfaced with a vengeance.

'You can have the room at the top of the steps,' she said, pointing though the hall, 'go put your bag in there.'

I noticed the stair carpet was threadbare as I followed her instructions to find the spare room. It was nothing like my childhood cell, just a standard second bedroom, with a single bed, a cupboard and bedside table. Floral curtains hung in front of nets at the window and a couple of cheap pictures tried but failed to liven up the yellowing anaglypta.

Dumping my bag on the bed, I rummaged for my toothbrush and toothpaste and went to clean my teeth in the adjacent bathroom. After rinsing my mouth out, I looked at my reflection in the mirror above the sink and running my fingers through my hair, stared closely at the scar she'd left just above my hairline. Her mark.

I began to question my motivation for being here. Was this what I expected? Could she have changed? Shaking my head, I made a mental note not to look back, to be the better person. Then I went back to the bedroom, put my wallet in my pocket and went downstairs. 'You weren't expecting me, so let's go out to eat,' I said.

She didn't protest. I rang for a taxi as she got changed, then we headed back into Blackpool. I felt an overwhelming need to tell her what I was doing with my life, and during the next few hours filled her in about my boyfriend Phil, whom I lived with in Harrogate, my full-time employment, and volunteering with St John Ambulance. I was earning, going places and moving forward. There wasn't a word of encouragement or pride from her.

I asked her about Luke and Claire, but she didn't seem too bothered about where they were or what they were doing. By this point, Claire would have been seventeen and Luke about twenty-one. She said she had a problem with her legs, which is why she needed a stick to walk and that she'd been living with Bernard for a while. She didn't offer any information on her former husband, the paedophile, and I didn't ask.

Towards the end of the meal, a certain old behaviour resurfaced. The way she looked at me when I casually glanced at her plate reminded me of how she'd force me to eat all her food too, if I'd dared to look up. I think she remembered as well, but there was no sense of shame.

I paid the bill and we got a taxi home, by which point, Bernard had arrived back and was sat in the lounge like a lummox.

'This is Bernard,' she said, pointing at him laid out on the sofa.' He looked across and said hello but didn't offer to shake my hand. He had no intention of getting up.

'Hi,' I said, and left it at that. I didn't owe him anything. My mother had obviously texted him at some point to tell him I'd turned up out of the blue.

Fortunately, it was quite late by this point, so I said I was ready for bed. I hung by the door for a second, then for some reason, suggested taking her food shopping the next day.

'Yeah, alright then,' she said.

'Night then,' I said, heading to the stairs.

'Okay' she said, walking over to the sofa without a backward glance. When I got to my room, I shut the bedroom door and leaning against it, breathed a sigh of relief. This pretend-normal was weird, but it would have to do for now. No major breakthroughs, apologies or explanations, but I was there, it was a start.

I didn't sleep easily, spending more time staring at the ceiling, wondering if I was doing the right thing. I knew she couldn't lock me in as I was physically much stronger than her, but it didn't stop me imagining what would happen if she did. In reality, I could use the toilet if I wanted to and if I got hungry, I could go downstairs and make myself some toast. But I didn't do either of those things.

When I got up in the morning, I was keen to leave the house as soon as possible. It was depressing.

Once she was dressed, I suggested heading straight to the shops. I think because she seemed so much older and had to use a walking stick, instinct kicked in, making me want to look after her. I know that sounds ridiculous after everything she put me through, but that's honestly how I felt. It was like wanting to make sure your grandma was alright – because that's how she seemed to me, like a frail old woman.

She filled her trolley to the brim. Disgustingly full. It felt like she was challenging me to tell her not to be so greedy, but I didn't rise to the bait. She could put what she wanted in. Her diabetes came as no surprise to me, seeing the amount of crap she chose. Hardly anything was fresh.

After I paid at the checkout, I bagged everything up and carried the lot back to the bus stop. She looked pleased with herself, like it had been her idea to lure me there so she could take, take, take. But I tried to dismiss it. Conversations remained neutral all the way home, where she suddenly got a burst of energy and managed to unpack everything herself – even reaching for the higher corner shelves. I watched her. Wondered what she'd do next.

Begrudgingly, she offered to make lunch. It was just some basic, bland food that she'd had left in the fridge. There was no treating me to any of the goods I'd just bought her, she was saving all that for herself. I walked into the lounge and, picking up the remote from the arm of the sofa where Bernard had left it the night before, I flicked on the television. I could hear my mother shuffling about in the kitchen, but I didn't offer to help with preparation. I felt I'd done enough for her already and knew she wasn't grateful.

There weren't any photographs in the house of her children. No memories of our youth. It was like none of us had ever existed. There didn't seem to be any of Bernard's family either and it got me wondering how they'd met – and how soon it was after my stepdad went to prison. Then there was a breaking newsflash, and footage of a massive tower on fire in New York. I sat forward and turned the volume up.

It looked like an aeroplane had crashed into it and there was smoke everywhere. It was chaos – people were running away from the scene, jumping from the top stories, sirens whirring into action. People were trapped. Nobody knew what was going on. Some were trying to squeeze into cars heading out of the area, others, just walking, stunned. Then there was another crash – and a second plane hit the second tower.

I couldn't believe what I was looking at and called my mother through to watch. She appeared in the doorway and just stared, passively. It was surreal. News reporters seemed incredulous as they shared what little knowledge they had about events unfolding before them. After a few minutes, my mother snuck away to my bedroom.

Eventually, she said lunch was ready, so I went to the kitchen and sat down at the table. I kept the volume up on the television so we could hear the rolling news. She was still looking pleased with herself, as if she knew something I didn't. But I just ignored it and carried on eating, making sure not to look too closely at her plate.

She still hadn't said sorry or mentioned anything about when I was growing up. I wanted to know how much she knew about my move to Farmlands and then to Newton Aycliffe. Had she heard I was forced into prostitution? Did she think it was me who started the fire with Brett? There were a lot of questions, but the time never seemed right to ask them. After lunch, I went upstairs to the toilet and when I came out of the bathroom, noticed my bedroom door was ajar. I peered around the corner and could see that my bag had been opened. When I got closer, it looked like it had been ransacked. All my stuff was messed up, some of my clothes spilling out on the bed. There was only one person who could have done this, and I was absolutely fuming. I ran back downstairs.

'Have you been through my bag?' I asked my mother.

'Yes'

'Why?'

'Well you're in my house,' she said calmly, 'I want to know what you're bringing in.' I didn't say another word. I went back upstairs, returned everything to my bag and stomped back down. I glared at her and kept walking towards the door.

'Don't go,' she said, hobbling after me.

But I couldn't answer her or look at her. I needed to get out of that house before I did something I'd regret. The woman hadn't changed. That woman, who did all those intolerable things to me as a child was still exactly the same and I couldn't bear to be near her a second longer. I'd given her an opportunity, a second chance, and she'd thrown it right back in my face.

It hurt, but I wasn't a little boy anymore. I was nearly twenty and in charge of my own destiny. She couldn't control me.

I didn't slam the door, just left it halfway open and walked down the path away from her evil, my head reeling with the reality of what she truly was. It felt like people in the street had realised too – there were looks of disbelief all around and people talking. It took me a while to figure out that they knew nothing about my mother, and they were discussing the twin towers catastrophe.

Just as I was approaching the bus stop, a double decker pulled up and I jumped on to get to the train station. I grabbed the nearest seat, and with my bag at my feet, stared out of the window, knowing I would never, ever contact my mother again. I felt emotionally raw and couldn't get away from Blackpool quickly enough. I wanted to put the whole incident behind me and swore that from then on, I was looking forward only.

I saw her one last time before she died, through circumstance, not choice. Even then, years later, she was still up to her old tricks.

20

•

Dogs and Debt

I WAS KEEN to get back to Phil in Harrogate so I could tell him everything that had happened in Blackpool. But when I arrived at the flat, he wasn't there and didn't pick up his mobile when I called and left messages. Then at around midnight, he stumbled in completely drunk. When he saw me sat on the sofa waiting for him, he looked very sheepish.

'Where've you been?' I asked.

'Rob and Marcus's house,' he slurred.

'Right. Well, I hope you had a good time while I was going through hell at my mother's.'

'You're back early. I'd have been back if I'd known.'

It was pointless discussing anything when he was so drunk. I was beginning to get suspicious of what he was up to with Rob and Marcus as he seemed to be spending a lot of time with them both. We'd all been out to the pub a few times, but I knew Rob and Marcus were into sex with more than one person – threesomes and orgies, which just weren't my scene and I wanted a relationship with someone who felt the same.

Phil walked through into the kitchen to find more alcohol and I went to bed. It was a crap end to a dispiriting couple of days. I'd really hoped that he would understand and be there for me, but when he was drunk, my feelings weren't his priority. It should have been a big red flag to get the hell out of there while I could.

The problem was that Phil was an alcoholic. When we first

got together it was fun to be out drinking all the time, but he never seemed to have an 'off' switch. At the end of the night, it was never enough to come home and go to bed, he'd always be looking for the next high either in a bottle or a wrap of drugs. But the escalation of his behaviour was so gradual that it became sort-of normal, easy to explain away to myself. I didn't like the situation but couldn't face leaving him.

I decided it would be a good idea to move a bit further out of town, to try a new place where temptation wasn't right on the doorstep. When I suggested it, Phil seemed keen too and by the following year, we'd rented a place in Boston Spa about twelve miles south of Harrogate, equidistant between York and Leeds.

Things were good again for a while. The house was a lovely tall end terrace, with a great long garden at the back. It was set over three floors with a large bathroom in the basement, a living room and kitchen on the ground floor and then up to two bedrooms at the top. It was quite countryfied and I loved making it feel like a home.

I had my twenty-first birthday party in the garden there, and it felt great to host a real mixture of people from my past and present, including Richard and a pal of his from work, my uncle Geoff and his daughters, and a handful of Phil's friends (which inevitably included Rob and Marcus). The sun shone, we had a barbeque, and everyone had a good time.

I began feeling like I could really start putting my past behind me. I was alive, in a relationship and employed. And after two or three years with St John Ambulance, I heard the NHS were looking for First Responders, so I completed their Category A emergency course and was accepted on the team. It was important to me to be in a role where I was putting others before me. The need to help people was my driving force way over and above any thoughts of a salary.

This time, there was no need for me to be 'buddied up' to ensure I wasn't a risk – I'd proven that beyond a shadow of a doubt with St John Ambulance. All the extra training with the NHS was fascinating, and I got a big kick out of using this new knowledge to help others. I realised that in someone's hour of need, my personal skills were just as important as my practical ones.

I'd come a long way since leaving the care system and felt grateful that in many ways I'd had a lucky escape. Then on 22nd January 2004, I was blindsided by some news about my brother Luke. He had been convicted of manslaughter.

Newspaper reports told of him stabbing his dentist 'lover' to death. He had apparently been living with this dentist – a man – who was thirty-seven years older than him. My brother had told the court that he was his 'rent boy' and been given jewellery and a car. He had even changed his surname by deed poll to the dentist's surname. He was sentenced to five years in jail.

I felt sick.

This was shocking in more ways than one. I couldn't believe my own brother had stabbed someone to death. I just kept wondering what he must have gone through to get to the stage where there was no other option. How and why had that relationship become so toxic? Had Luke, like me, experienced layer upon layer of abuse at the children's home where he'd been placed – at Red Tiles? You hear of very few murderers with no prior history of violence or major turmoil in their lives.

But also surprising was the fact that he'd had a gay lover. He never admitted to being gay when we were younger. Of the handful of times Luke and I met up at Wollaton Park with social workers from our respective care homes, he seemed to blame my homosexuality on a lot of his problems at Red Tiles. He said other kids called him names because they'd heard I was a 'rent boy' and he wanted me to stop.

Was the sexual aspect of this relationship forced? Learned behaviour from previous abuses? The dentist was nearly sixty and Luke was in his early twenties, that didn't seem right to me. The Roger situation sprang to mind. I just don't believe my brother is gay. But I also don't believe the dentist deserved to be killed, and my heart goes out to his family.

The Judge must have heard something in that courtroom to let my brother off with just a five-year prison sentence for such a horrendous murder. The news of it was a hugely life-altering moment for me, one which I discussed at length with Gary, Pauline, Richard and Anna. Phil though, didn't step up to support me. He assumed it was just collateral damage for some kids brought up in a failing care system.

While I gradually tried to process the fact that my brother was a murderer, Phil threw his energy into setting up his own employment agency, breaking away from the safety of a steady job. In theory, it was a good idea and I supported him when he took an office space in Wetherby.

But he was never fully focused on the job because he was a functioning alcoholic. As time went on, he became more and more stressed about the failure of his business, which made him reach for the bottle more often and before I knew it, he was a fully blown addict, looking for alternative ways to supplement his income.

Pauline, yet again, sensed something was up and when Phil and I went to visit her, she pulled me to one side when Phil went to the bathroom.

'Are you alright?' she asked.

'Yeah, fine,' I replied.

'Are you sure?' she pushed 'Are you one hundred percent comfortable in this relationship?'

'I think I'm just trying to work things out, Pauline.'

'Well, son, if you do not feel comfortable with this relationship that you're in, you have to be honest,' she said.

I couldn't express how I felt about what was happening. It was only when I was with her and other close friends, that I could properly measure the extent of it, and see how abnormal my relationship was becoming.

When Phil returned from the toilet, we got ready to leave.

Maybe I'd gone to Pauline's with Phil because I was subconsciously searching for her opinion, knowing things weren't right. 'You take care now,' she said to us both.

Pauline leaned in and gave Phil a small, cursory hug, then wrapped me in a bear hug and whispered in my ear.

'You always know where I am, son.' I did know.

The journey back to Boston Spa was frosty. I think Phil knew Pauline was on to him and took umbridge when she hugged me for much longer than him. It was a while before I finally broke free from him though, trying every last trick in the book to make it work, against all warnings.

Phil had been trying to engage me in group sex with him, Rob and Marcus. He said it would be fun and nothing to worry about, completely normal between consenting adults. But it just didn't float my boat. To keep Phil happy though, I agreed to go to Rob's house and play it by ear, just join in if I wanted to. It was obviously something that none of them were prepared to do stone cold sober, so there was plenty of alcohol flowing.

Then one of them put a video in and it was of the three of them doing all sorts to each other, my hunch was right, this had been going on for a long time. I kind-of knew, but faced with actual footage, I couldn't kid myself anymore. I felt uncomfortable with the whole scenario, but the three of them were obviously getting turned on and began emulating what was happening on the screen. Phil looked over at me and encouraged me to take part.

'Come on, you might enjoy it,' he said, 'Just try it, *for me.*'

I reluctantly joined them, and he was wrong. I didn't enjoy it but I carried on, to please him. It made me feel used and exploited, taking me right back to my youth.

These other guys couldn't have cared less who I was. To them, I was a piece of meat in the middle of an orgy, whom they could do whatever they liked with.

There were no loving moments, no questions about whether I was happy with this or that. It was horrendous and I couldn't wait for it to end.

When they were all done, I left Phil there and made my way back to our place feeling dirty and miserable. I needed him to know that I wasn't happy and never wanted to be coerced into that situation again. This was exactly what I didn't want my life to be.

When I got home, I rang Anna.

She said that it wasn't typical behaviour, that it was only alright if everyone was happy with the situation, and if nobody was being paid for it. From a very young age, I'd been forced into sexualised behaviour and as such, I sometimes didn't see through the blurred lines as clearly as others. I knew it wasn't right but needed confirmation and Anna provided that for me.

Like an idiot though, instead of running for the hills, I tried to change him. I thought that if our relationship was official, then he would fully commit to just me.

We had a civil ceremony at the Registry Office in Harrogate, followed by a meal at Hotel du Vin. My friends and some of those close to me came, but none of Phil's family were there. I loved the fact that people saw us making a commitment to each other. It felt like a big step, like I was an adult with all the trappings which came with that. I even took his last name.

As best man, Richard hoped that we'd be able to make a go of things, but now admits he wasn't completely comfortable on the day. Anna struggled because she could see Phil's heart wasn't in it. She thought he was more bothered about where his next can of lager was coming from than taking care of me and didn't like the way he got more and more lairy as the day drew on. Her friends, Heather and Becky, agreed.

Predictably, not much changed relationship-wise after our so-called big day, but something happened not long after which enhanced my working life forever.

I'd taken in a couple of rescue dogs a few months earlier, and when I was out with them one day, a lady approached me and asked how much I charged per hour for dog-walking. Off the top of my head, I said ten pounds, and that's when the earlier seed planted at the kennels and cattery began to take root.

Boston Spa is an affluent area, so there are plenty of people with pets who work full-time. After getting some flyers together, I did a leaflet-drop around the houses to offer my services as a dog walker. Take up was better than I could have imagined, and I soon had enough dogs on my books to turn it into a proper job.

It seemed like such a natural thing to do because I love caring for animals and enjoy being in the outdoors. My business, The Dog Walker, was born. I was now my own boss. With that, I felt more in control of my own destiny and my confidence grew. When we moved to a cottage in Bramham soon after, it was easy to keep my clients from Boston Spa and add more there. I was very busy.

Unfortunately, my growing success coincided with Phil's deeper descent into alcoholism as his business spiraled downwards. He was looking into other avenues to fund his habits and began trying to coerce me back into prostitution – an activity I never chose for myself in the first place. He knew about my past, so in his alcoholic mind, he thought I'd find it easy to return to that way of life and pattern of abuse. He couldn't have been more wrong.

This was a different scenario to when I'd been forced into sex acts with other men by Kevin and Brett. I did those because, as a fearful little boy, I literally had no choice. With Phil, he was emotionally manipulating me. He didn't use fear and violence, he guilt-tripped me, making me believe it was my fault that he'd turned to drugs and alcohol, and it was the least I could do to help him climb out of debt.

Phil found customers via a website called Gaydar. When sober, he was very computer-savvy and good at design, so in no time at all he set up a profile called Two Lads Rent, and basically managed it like a pimp would. He made out like he was doing me a favour by joining in as well, offering specialisms in group sex.

Our relationship ended not long after that. It had taken years for the penny to drop that this guy wasn't good for me. Like so many others before, he'd seen me as a cash cow and didn't care about me one bit. It all came to a halt after a blazing row one night, when I refused to take part in any more prostitution. He was so furious he threw a cup at my head, leaving a scar close to the one my mum created when she smashed my head against the wooden step.

I'd also begun to suspect he had another boyfriend. Prior to the civil ceremony, we often house-sat for his parents when they were away. But he'd stopped asking me to go with him. When I questioned why, he fobbed me off with an excuse so lame I can't even remember it, so I waited until the next time he went and followed him. He'd been seeing a man a couple of doors down from his parents'.

Richie – Who Cares?

There was nothing left between us. I'd exhausted every single avenue trying to make 'us' work and come to the end of the line, so when Phil returned from his parent's house, there was a hire van waiting outside ours.

'Get your stuff in that van and fuck off,' I said.

He didn't argue. But he did leave me with thirty thousand pounds worth of debt. In the early days of his business, Phil had asked me to sign a few documents and because I trusted him, I just did it without question. My name was a guarantor for his company, and it was me who had to deal with creditors and sort out the whole mess. It took years.

He'd coerced me sexually and financially and left me with nothing. I was devastated that my civil partnership had broken down and felt like a total failure. All I wanted was a stable, trusting relationship but I'd been instead flogging a dead horse for the best part of six years.

After moping about the house and feeling sorry for myself for a few months, I eventually concluded that I'd overcome worse. If I was one thing, it was resilient. But I needed a friend, and I wanted some fun – so I rang Richard.

We went to Brussels on the Eurostar for a weekend and it was brilliant. During the day, we did a bit of sightseeing – the Grand Place and the Europa building, we ate in nice cafes and soaked up the atmosphere. At night though, because Richard is a bit older than me and not fussed about clubbing, he went back to the hotel, and I headed out on the town.

One night I returned to the room with absolutely no recollection of how I'd got back. I just knew I'd met a bunch of fun people and had a ball. Richard enjoyed hearing about all the places I'd been to (that I could remember) and those I chatted with. He loved seeing me grasping life with both hands and felt I'd earned the chance to let my hair down.

On another occasion, we went to Edinburgh, and he still tells the tale of when I bought us a couple of cinema tickets but scrimped by getting him a senior citizen's one. He blew a gasket, but it was so funny. He flatly refused to watch the film because he said it was unethical to buy the wrong ticket and he was clearly not a senior citizen. I went on my own and we both laughed about it later.

Once Phil was out of my life, I enjoyed the freedom of living on my own in Boston Spa. I was keeping myself busy and building up The Dog Walker, looking at the possibility of expanding it into a franchising business. There seemed to be an appetite for it because in 2007, not many people were doing what I was. I got there right at the start.

I began to focus on my physical fitness too. It hadn't been a priority with Phil as he was more about abusing his body instead of improving it. So maybe it was because I was in that mindset, that I was drawn to another man, who turned out to be a personal trainer.

Dean couldn't have been more different to Phil. We met online and he was a kind, motivated guy. It felt like all my birthdays had come at once and it didn't take long for us to establish a relationship. He'd been renting a room in Baildon, West Yorkshire, but his wages weren't great, so after spending most of our time at my place, we decided it made sense for him to move in with me in Bramham.

I still wanted to keep some things about my past private though. After the way Phil used that knowledge to coerce me into prostitution, my barriers stayed up. I still felt vulnerable and didn't want this new relationship tarnished by my childhood circumstances. I wanted him to treat me like any normal guy.

Our first Christmas together was lovely, but I started feeling a bit under the weather soon after, like I had a cold that I couldn't shift and a bad chest. Then I noticed similarities in the symptoms to when I was living in Shipley about seven years before. But this nosedived suddenly, creating so much pressure on my heart and lungs that I found it difficult to breathe. It was like I'd been hit by a freight train.

After tossing and turning all night, fretting and unable to sleep, my heart started tightening and I properly panicked. I was still working with the NHS First Response team at this point, so had half an idea about what it could be and called 111. The woman at the other end asked about my symptoms and then told me what was going to happen. 'Listen love, an ambulance will be with you very soon. You're having a heart attack.'

Not the news you want to hear, but I knew there were varying degrees of this, so didn't think death was imminent. Nonetheless, it was frightening. I was still just in my boxer shorts and even though Dean knew something was going on, he wasn't too concerned. He thought I was being dramatic and went back to sleep. I just about managed to get to the front door to unlock it and then slumped by the side, waiting for help.

I vaguely remember the blue lights flashing and being carried into the back of the ambulance. I was rushed to York Hospital, straight to Accident & Emergency, where they transferred me into a wheelchair – at which point I had another heart attack. The matron on duty saw me and spoke to one of the team.

'This another party boy is it? Someone needing somewhere to stay?'

'No. This is serious. He needs to get to CCU (Cardiac Care Unit) now,' the medic replied.

I was there for a week. They pumped me full of fluids and antibiotics and insisted on bed rest. All manner of tests were done, and it transpires I have a lifelong condition called myocardial pericarditis. It's basically an inflammation of the heart, so if the flu virus attacks my body, it attacks my heart and swells it to almost twice the size, increasing pressure on it and my lungs. You can imagine how paranoid I was when Covid-19 arrived on the scene. As soon as the vaccines were rolled out, I couldn't wait to get jabbed.

Dean came to visit me in hospital the next morning. It was good to see him, but my main concern was not wanting to let my dog walking customers down. If I didn't turn up, the animals would be shut in the house all day. I asked Dean if he would step in and do the rounds and by the end of the week, he realised he could earn a lot more walking dogs than he could do as a personal trainer, so when I was well enough to go home, we talked about the idea of him working for me.

Over time, I ended up giving Dean half of one of my franchises in the area. I concentrated on Wetherby, Boston Spa,

Bramham and Clifford. Dean took Thorner, Bardsey, Collingham and the other side of Wetherby. I bought his van, his equipment and handed the clients over. I naively didn't create a contract.

For a good few years, our relationship bobbed along without incident. I'd introduced him to the important people in my life and they seemed to warm to him. I always got the impression that Dean's parents wanted me to prove myself though, like I wasn't good enough for their son. There weren't any arguments between us, but I felt an underlying sense of never being fully accepted.

It was around about this point when I started having regular nightmares. I think it was because I was still holding so much in about my childhood, not addressing the full impact of what I'd been through. It didn't take much for me to get stressed if small things needed ironing out at work because to me, my business was a marker of my escape from my youth. I couldn't let that fail. Little issues manifested themselves into major crisis in my dreams as they intermingled with previous trauma. They were exacerbated by having to come face to face with my mother again.

The meeting was at my uncle Geoff's wedding in August 2009, where I was Best Man. Even though Dean was by my side, it wasn't a day either of us would want to keep in a memory box. Dean didn't know anybody and I spent most of the time avoiding conflict with my mother.

Part of my wedding present to the happy couple was to be their driver for the day. I've always loved nice cars, and because my business was doing well, had recently treated myself to a Mercedes Benz. I made sure it was immaculate inside and out and trimmed the bonnet with ribbon. It looked fantastic and they both absolutely loved it.

Apart from my brother and sister, most of the extended family were there – but none of them had much time for me. I briefly chatted to my grandad, Geoff's wife and her little daughter, and a couple of my cousins. But most conversations were pretty surface, focusing firmly on the present. My mother could see I was still doing well and tried her hardest to get my attention, no doubt seeing me as a meal ticket once more. But I wanted nothing to do with her after the bag incident in Blackpool. She'd shown me she hadn't changed one single bit and I wasn't falling for a sob story. She even resorted to grabbing my arm, causing a scene with other relatives by saying I wouldn't talk to her and I was upsetting her.

But when nobody was paying my mother enough attention, she went a step too far. Using one of her crutches, she made a massive scratch in the bonnet of my car. She'd run out of ways to verbally or physically abuse me, so applied the only tool she had left. She didn't give a crap that it was Geoff's big day, that she might spoil it with her childish tantrums.

But although Geoff was pissed off with her behaviour, I think it made him realise what his sister was really like. She'd shown her true colours. Strangely, her actions left me feeling like I'd won because she'd finally lost her grip over me. She couldn't face the fact that I was successful, happy and free.

I kept in touch with Geoff a reasonable amount after the wedding because he was my one link to the rest of my family. I'd tried to form relationships with my mum's other sisters but they weren't interested. I was also in contact with one of their sons on Facebook for a while, but that never went anywhere. It was through Geoff that I found out my sister's first two children had been taken off her for abuse issues. Suspicious bruising had been found.

I'd also heard that my mother was trying to get custody of them and I hit the roof. I got straight on to Blackpool Council stating that under no circumstances were those children to be in my mother's unsupervised care. I've no idea if it was my intervention that swung things but do know they never lived with my mother.

Claire went on to have four children altogether, but the second two were adopted at birth. My mother wanted to look after those as well but the powers that be saw sense. Thank God.

I have lodged my details as a family member at Blackpool Council and expressed a wish that when Claire's children come of age, if they want to find me, then I would love that. But the ball is in their court. At least they have the option. I just hope that they have a happy, stable upbringing with adoptive parents who love them and give them every chance in life.

21

•

Roots and Ben

IN 2011, DEAN and I decided to buy a house together in Sherburn in Elmet in North Yorkshire. I'd finally paid off all the debt that Phil left me and had started building up a nice little nest egg for the future. I was sick of paying rent and wanted permanent roots.

Dean wasn't as far along the line in terms of savings, so he borrowed his half of the deposit from his parents and we put both our names on the mortgage. Because Dean didn't earn as much as me, we decided that I would take on all the payments of the house and he would contribute a couple of hundred pounds a month towards our bills. We agreed that I would eventually pay his parents his part of the deposit back. Both of us were happy with that arrangement.

It felt good to have a solid base just twenty minutes' drive from our old pad, meaning I could keep The Dog Walker clients we already had, and look to expand in the area. My life was feeling as settled as I'd ever known it, though the nightmares weren't improving.

About a year after we were properly settled into our new home, Dean started cheating on me. He had a friend in London whom we often went down to see. This friend worked at the restaurant in the Oxo Tower and rented a room from a guy who worked on a shopping channel. Sometimes, Dean went to London on his own, claiming to be visiting his sister and honestly, I didn't spot the signs. Even when we went to London together and his friend was very tactile with Dean, I just thought that was the way he was. I began to suspect something after Dean and I were offered the chance to join a group of people on a skiing holiday in Solden, Austria, and Dean said he didn't want to go, that he might just go to London instead. I really wanted to go skiing again so went without him and had an absolute blast. Our accommodation was basic, but the scenery and pistes were magnificent.

There were just five of us in the group and we were all at different levels of skiing ability. The last time I'd been on the slopes was when I was sixteen, just before I left Newton Aycliffe, so I booked in for a few sessions at the indoor slope at Xscape in Castleford beforehand to get back into the swing of it. It was like riding a bike and once I got to Austria, I fully went for it. I even dared to go down a black run and didn't fall over.

Towards the end of the trip, I received a message from the housemate of Dean's friend, telling me that they were in a relationship. I was obviously upset, but that holiday showed me there was more to life than Dean. I had to accept that we'd been drifting apart for a while and think we both knew deep down that ultimately, we weren't going to make each other happy for the rest of our lives. When I returned form Solden, we decided to go our separate ways.

I still cared about Dean though and wasn't going to just boot him out of the house. I wanted to make sure he had somewhere else to live first, and I'd planned to sort out a proper contract for him for The Dog Walker franchise, so he'd still be earning. We moved into separate bedrooms but were still on speaking terms.

Dean and I spent a lot of time avoiding each other, and most evenings I holed up in my bedroom watching *Star Trek* DVDs and scrolling through Facebook. I was following an open forum about the TV series *Family Guy*, and someone 'liked' one of my comments, so we ended up having a bit of banter about the show. Then one of his pals, Ben, started chiming in with his opinions and he seemed completely on my wavelength.

My conversations with Ben got friendlier and after a while, we came off the open forum and began talking privately. I checked out some of his photos and thought tall, muscly, strong jawline, gorgeous eyes and a real twinkly smile. Very handsome. I told him about my situation with Dean, how we were living in the same house but not together anymore. He told me that he was in a relationship but they didn't cohabit and it was waning. We found we had a lot in common and really enjoyed chatting to each other. We had a laugh, talked openly, and gradually became friends.

It was refreshing to feel so at ease with someone and even though I didn't lay everything on the table straight away, I got the sense that if I did want to share my history with Ben, he would be respectful. But it cut both ways. Without realising it, Ben was also looking for that missing element of understanding and in each other, we seemed to find it.

Every time I spoke to Ben, I felt lighter, happier, bubbly even. Naturally, the gaps between online contact grew shorter and we eventually agreed to meet at his flat in Jarrow, Tyne & Wear.

It was clear there was an attraction for both of us, but Ben was very honest. He told me he wasn't looking for a relationship because he was still entangled with his boyfriend but would struggle to let me go in terms of friendship. I also felt that while I was still under the same roof as Dean, I didn't want to jump straight into another full-on deal. We agreed to be friends with benefits.

As much as I loved the physical element, the friendship side of things was equally thrilling. We began spending more and more time doing things we both enjoyed – just out and about socialising in bars, going to the cinema, restaurants and generally hanging out more. I felt relaxed when I was with Ben and, in our quieter moments, began to open up about my childhood.

Ben impressed me no end with the way he accepted my truth. Having previously worked for the job centre, then with ex-offenders and vulnerable people, he was well-placed to listen to some of the horrors I endured with an open heart and mind. He did his best to try and make me see that none of it was my fault and encouraged me to keep talking. I could feel that he wanted to know more so he could understand me better.

By July, people started gossiping about us. We had nothing to hide though. We were cool with what we were doing and didn't feel the need to explain ourselves to anyone. We found comfort and companionship in each other.

It sounds weird, but Dean was fine with it all. So much so that when Ben came to my house before going to Betty's Café for afternoon tea, the pair of them shook hands and were civil with each other. It was clear to everyone that my relationship with Dean was absolutely, completely over.

By September, Ben had broken things off with his boyfriend and we became an official couple. It felt amazing. I couldn't believe my luck and wanted everyone to know. It was still a bit tricky on the home front though because Dean hadn't moved out yet, but that was only a matter of time. Ben made me happier than I'd ever been, and life was really looking up.

He introduced me to some of his family. I'd heard a lot about them, and they sounded great. He spoke fondly about his mum and his Nana and the rest of his siblings. He'd grown up in a loving family, playing freely with his brothers, with food on the table every day and a clean uniform for school. I was nervous they wouldn't understand why my childhood had been so different.

I met them at his mum's house, but my problem is that I have a tendency to go over the top with people I don't know well. Nervous energy makes me talk ten to the dozen and I always feel the need to impress or justify myself. So sometimes, I come across all wrong, like I'm boasting about my achievements, but it's not meant to sound like that. I guess it's because deep down I'm always trying to distance myself from my past, and if people can see I'm doing well, they won't think I'm like the rest of the kids in the care homes who keep hitting the headlines. I just want to appear like a normal, well-adjusted adult.

I was so keen for Ben's family to like me that I went completely overboard, I was manic. They must have wondered what on earth Ben was doing with me, particularly when I went gushing over to his Auntie Pam and laid it on really thick. I was like a kid in a sweet shop, five steps ahead of everybody else in the room, already imagining them as my own relatives. They were more than a little bit wary, even though Ben had told them snippets about my upbringing. But I don't think they were prepared for me being so full-on.

I wouldn't say I completely blew it, but I had to admit that I should have eased off a bit. When I went to visit Ben a couple of months later, that meeting with his family played on my mind as I left his flat. Did I simply not know how to handle myself? Why couldn't I read the social cues? What the hell was wrong with me?

I'd finished work for the week – all my customer's dogs had been fed, walked and were happy, so it was with a light heart that I drove the usual 100 miles to Jarrow. But after an initial passionate greeting, I could tell things weren't right. He just seemed on edge, distant, like he needed to get something off his chest. I decided to keep my mouth shut and wait to see if anything developed and, unfortunately, it did.

Ben cleared his throat. 'I'm really enjoying spending all this time with you Richie. It's amazing that we get on so well and have so much in common. But I have to be honest.'

My stomach dropped.

'My partner is practically begging me to take him back,' he continued. 'He wants a fresh start. We've been together for seven years and I still love him, can't seem to get him out of my system.'

I wasn't prepared for this at all. Ben must have seen it in my face because he just kept talking.

'I'm so sorry, but I've just got to give it a go with him because if I don't, I'll never know.'

Silence.

'But I don't want to let you go as a friend. Could we still be friends – but without benefits? Could that work?'

My heart was hammering in my chest, and it took a moment for me to gather my thoughts.

'Do you really believe him? Do you honestly think he means it when he says he wants to be with you?' I asked.

'I do,' he said.

This was killing me. I was so cross that Ben was being prised away from me and felt sure the only reason his ex wanted him now, was because someone else did. But I knew above all else, that I didn't want Ben to slip through my fingers. I couldn't bear the thought of never seeing him again and if it was friendship or nothing, then I'd take friendship for now and keep hoping this other guy would eventually trip himself up. I looked at Ben and tried to smile.

'If friendship is all you can offer, then friendship it is,' I said.

Ben exhaled. He'd obviously been building up to this moment and was relieved I hadn't kicked off or given him an ultimatum. Even though I was hurting like hell, the last thing I wanted to do was cause him angst. I understood that if he loved his partner, he needed to give it another go. He'd been honest about his feelings, and I had to respect that, but it was tough.

'Thank you,' he said.

I managed to hold it together when we had a 'friends' hug outside his flat. I even kept the tears at bay during my walk back to the car, but after unlocking the door and plonking down in the drivers' seat, I couldn't bring myself to turn around and wave goodbye. I put the car in gear and drove away, crumbling inside.

There was no denying I was jealous of his boyfriend. Why should *he* get a second chance? Ben had told me all about how he treated him, and it made my blood boil. This other guy was messing with his head, promising but never delivering, leaving him dangling for a nugget of affection and only showing interest when Ben was having a better time elsewhere. I knew that wasn't love. I also realised that what I was feeling for Ben almost certainly was.

It's a miracle I got home without crashing because once the floodgates were open, there was no stemming the flow of tears. Four songs on my iPod threatened to tip me over the edge and I still can't hear them without welling up. One of them was 'Happy' by Marina and The Diamonds, then George Michael's 'A Different Corner', Naughty Boy's 'Running' and Sigma's 'Find Me'. By the time I reached my front door I was a wreck, having sobbed all the way from Jarrow to Sherburn in Elmet.

My head was all over the place and the only thing I wanted to do was lay on my bed and figure out this tangle of emotions. I knew I'd fallen for Ben, but this situation wasn't just about me. I had to put what I wanted to one side and try to think of it from his point of view. I wanted to be the person to Ben who Gary, Pauline, Anna and Richard had been to me. Always there, always supporting, whatever the situation.

The next day, I rang Richard to talk everything through and as usual, he didn't say, 'you should do this or that', but just listened, digested it, then threw a load of questions back at me to help me come to my own conclusions. He asked why I felt so bothered about Ben, what I thought Ben's feelings were towards me in comparison to the other guy – and where I would ideally like the relationship to go.

Richard gave me the space to vent my frustration without judgement, encouraging me to look critically at why my feelings for Ben might be different to those I'd had at the start of other long-term relationships. By verbalising my thoughts and emotions about him, I became more comfortable with my decision to step back and just be friends. I knew I wanted to stick around regardless.

I'm glad I did.

A couple of months later, Ben got a terrible chest infection and had to take a lot of time off work. For some of that, he was left without sick pay while still living on his own. The so-called boyfriend didn't step up when Ben needed to go to the doctor or collect antibiotics. As soon as I realised he wasn't being looked after, I drove to Jarrow, went food shopping for him, made soup and left him the equivalent of a few days sick pay. All this time, his partner was just three stops away on the Metro and didn't check in.

In the run up to Christmas, as his boyfriend continued to keep him dangling, I went to Ben's flat and was bowled over. He'd bought me loads of little presents, each one really thoughtful and wrapped beautifully. He said when I first began talking about my childhood, he was so saddened at the thought of what my Christmases must have been like, that he just wanted to make this one good for me.

When he was growing up, his mum always reminded him that some children weren't lucky enough to get presents from their parents. He couldn't cope with the fact that I used to be one of those little boys. He took my breath away. Honestly, he could have wrapped up empty matchboxes and I wouldn't have felt any less love for him at that moment. The sentiment behind what he did meant so much and I knew I had to be by his side in whatever shape or form that took.

It was April by the time Dean moved out without warning. He waited until I was away for the weekend then, with his family, completely cleared me out, taking everything apart from my office kit and his nine Bengal cats. They took sofas, pictures, crockery – even the kettle. He took my client records for The Dog Walker district I'd given him and the van I'd bought him. He even demanded a further ten thousand pounds.

It was galling to say the least, but once he began behaving like that, I just wanted him out of my life. I could have been an absolute bastard and taken him to the cleaners, but I let it go and can hold my head high. It was a valuable lesson, and I knew I would never be taken for granted in a relationship again.

Once that was sorted, I breathed a huge sigh of relief. It wasn't doing either of us any good with him still being around and although it wasn't ideal having to buy new things for the house again, in a way, it felt like a fresh start. It was great to have the space to myself and I began to relax again.

With an empty house, more opportunities arose for Ben and I to spend time together. It was killing me that we were still just friends, but I was right to remain a steady presence in his life. It was only a matter of months before his so-called boyfriend slipped back into his old ways and as things came to a head for them, they split again. I could see Ben was hurting but didn't want to push it in case I drove him away. I needn't have worried.

In June, Ben rented his flat out in Jarrow and moved in with me as a friend, which soon developed. In July, we became a proper item again. I felt so happy that things between us were moving in the right direction once more. Finally, he'd realised his ex was bad news and I was not.

Almost immediately, Ben's mettle was put to the test when I turned to him for advice about my sister, Claire.

She was trying to blackmail me.

22

•

Banishing the Past

CLAIRE SAID that unless I paid her a lot of money, she'd go to the newspapers and tell them all about me being a rent boy – a story she believed would ruin my business. It was both upsetting and worrying. I was gutted she would do something like that. If she'd been in real financial trouble, I would have helped her, but I knew she didn't want the cash for food and bills, she was after a spending spree on something that wouldn't have done anyone any good.

Claire saw that I was making a go of my life – supporting myself and putting my traumatic childhood behind me. She knew I was earning well after I showered her with gifts for her first-born. But it's hard to put into words how much of an impact a damaged upbringing can have on the rest of your life. Our stepdad's sexual abuse, coupled with my mother's twisted manipulation of our family left Claire with no confidence or self-worth, so I partly understood that she may have felt she had no other option to get money. But I couldn't accept that she was prepared to ruin my life for her gain.

I felt thrown by her demands and wondered if she might be right about me losing clients once they knew about my past. Would they understand? Or would they see me in a completely different light and only read the 'rent boy' headlines? Many of my customers have children, so would they perceive me as a risk to them? Claire had forced my mind back to my youth and brought a dilemma to my door. I was so proud of the business I'd built up and genuinely feared the rug being pulled from under my feet.

If I gave her the money though, would it end there? I spoke to Ben at length about the situation and our gut reactions were not to give in, but we decided to get a third opinion from Gary, who we met for lunch later that week. Gary listened to the predicament and tossed around some possible solutions. His advice was good.

'Richie, you haven't done anything wrong. Nothing that happened in your past is your fault. You have nothing to be ashamed of. Call her bluff,' he said.

Gary confirmed what we'd been thinking, and he was right in that I had absolutely nothing to hide. But there was something inside me that wanted to go one step further to quash any chance of her trying to wheedle more out of me in the future, so I took the bull by the horns and went to the press myself. I rang the local paper she'd been threatening to 'tip off' and then I did a double page spread in *Gay Times* magazine all about my childhood and how despite the odds, I'd built up The Dog Walker from nothing.

I haven't heard from her since.

My mother fleeced me when I visited her in Blackpool, then Claire tried to blackmail me, but the most shocking request for cash came from my brother Luke later that summer. Nearly fourteen years after he killed a dentist, he rang me out of the blue. He'd been out of prison for at least nine years, but only now decided to pick up the telephone. After a brief 'hello' he cut straight to the chase.

'There's nobody to pay for mum's funeral,' he said.

'What?'

Not one person in my family had bothered to inform me of her death. 'I didn't even know she'd died. What happened? When?'

'She collapsed on the street about two months ago,' he said.

'Two months ago?'

This was a lot to take in.

'Yeah.'

'Oh. Right,' I said.

'So will you pay for the funeral?'

Pardon? My brother was asking me to pay for the funeral of a woman who at every opportunity had tried to ruin my life both physically and mentally. The monster who locked me in a cold bedroom with no carpet, no curtains, no blankets, no light and no food for days on end? The torturer who rammed tablespoons of burning chilli powder down my throat and forced my brother to eat a plate of cigarette ends? The mother who turned a blind eye to her daughter being sexually abused by our stepdad, then lied and had us all sent to children's homes?

I was completely lost for words. And fuming.

'No. I won't pay for the funeral,' I managed to spit out.

'What do you mean, *no*? Everybody else is skint. You're the only one with cash. You'll have to pay.'

'I'm not paying one penny. She doesn't deserve a thing. She can rot in hell,' I said.

Luke's breathing got heavier as he tried to keep his temper under control. We'd spent less than two minutes on the phone, and he was already losing it.

'They can't move her from the morgue until someone pays, so you better fucking cough up or I'll fucking kill you.'

My own brother, a convicted murderer, threatening to kill me. What do you say to that? The answer is nothing.

I hung up and haven't heard from him since.

I still don't know who paid in the end. I don't know where the funeral was, whether she was buried or cremated. I don't want to sound heartless, but after what she did to me, I couldn't care less where her remains are. On the evening of that phone call, I went out and bought a bottle of Verve Cliquot champagne and celebrated with Ben.

'Good riddance,' we clinked.

Time to well and truly move on.

Ben was becoming fully aware of what my family were really like – and amazingly, he was still with me. I was learning how it felt to be loved and as a consequence, saw with clarity what I'd missed out on growing up. But my mother's death and subsequent mental throwback to my childhood meant my nightmares were growing ever more vivid and frequent.

I was waking up in sheer panic with images of my mother doing terrible things to me or kidnapping scenarios all mixed in with my current life. It was horrific, but the comfort of Ben holding me, telling me everything was going to be alright was overwhelming. Sometimes I'd just sob in his arms at the relief of waking up, knowing that my life had changed, and I never had to go back to my childhood.

In November 2015 I proposed to Ben. It wasn't your standard 'will you marry me?' moment on one knee with a ring in my hand, but it was certainly passionate and full of feeling and what matters is that he said yes. Loudly.

I woke up the next morning feeling like the luckiest man alive. Not wanting to break the spell, I very carefully turned to face him as he continued sleeping and just drank him in with my eyes. This handsome, kind, thoughtful man actually wanted to spend the rest of his life with me.

Where should we get married? Who should we invite? What about Best Men and Bridesmaids? I wanted the day to be so special. I had thoughts of castles, towering cakes, luxury rooms for our guests. There was so much to discuss and plan, people to share the good news with and I couldn't wait to see their faces. Pauline – or Mamma – as I'd called her now for years, would be thrilled. She'd already met Ben and the pair of them clicked straight away. I wanted her sons, David and Alfonzso and her sister, Odeth there. I wanted Gary to see me tying the knot with someone who truly loved me, for Anna to know that I was finally happy. I could already picture Richard with a little tear in his eye.

I was going to be part of Ben's family. A place where both of us would now belong, where Christmas's and birthdays were celebrated with love and happiness. The pair of us would grow old and grey, get grumpy and infirm, but we'd still be side by side, waking up and going to sleep next to each other. I was even looking forward to the boring bits where we watched a bit of tv or snoozed away a rainy Sunday afternoon.

Before any of that though, we had a holiday booked in Australia. I was going for a month and Ben was joining me for the second two weeks. We were staying with Heather and Becky, who had moved out there a few years before. I loved Australia and relished spending time with the girls again. It was a real bonus to get some sunshine in the middle of our winter and I was really excited about being with Ben for the last fortnight.

But Ben's ex took the opportunity to try and get back into his head while I was away. More ridiculous mind games ensued whereby Ben was almost being lured away from me with strings of lies and empty promises. I was sent screenshots of Ben's whereabouts by his ex, which understandably, put me in a spin, so by the time Ben arrived in Australia, there was tension.

Ben and I tried to talk things through and made the most of our time together, but I couldn't relax, always wondering if he truly wanted to be with me. It was psychological torture and made both of us behave in ways we're not proud of. When we got back to the UK, we called off the wedding. It couldn't work with this outside pressure in the background. I loved Ben with all my heart and soul, but the only way I could see us remaining friends was to try my hardest to keep my head and my cool.

A chaotic, highly emotional couple of months followed, with Ben still living with me but not being my partner. There was a lot to discuss and work through, but I felt the only thing I could do was let matters run their course. After thirty-three years on this planet, the most valuable lesson I'd learned was that you can't make someone else love you. They either do or they don't and the last thing I wanted to do was start behaving like Ben's ex. I thought if real love meant letting Ben go, then that's what I'd have to do.

By mid-February, it was clear that all the mudslinging from his ex was failing to stick and finally, Ben saw the light and told him to get out of his life forever. This time, I knew it was different for Ben because he was more angry than upset. Angry at being duped. He'd seen him for what he truly was – a user.

I tried my hardest to appear casual about the news, offering a shoulder to cry on and an attentive ear, but inside, I was flying. Still though, I kept my distance, knowing that if anything were to develop between us again, it had to come from Ben.

It was spring when he eventually broached the subject and, although I was cautious, I agreed. We had an amazing summer, which involved a big bash for his 40th with family and friends, and over the next nine months he proved to me that there was no going back. We moved house in November 2017 and then surprised everyone by throwing our complicated wedding plans out of the window and got hitched on holiday in New York on Christmas Day.

There'd been all the usual dramas in the run up to our previously planned nuptials. Not everyone was happy about the situation, the bridesmaid's dresses weren't the right colour and on top of it all, it was going to cost a fortune to host it at Hazelwood Castle, my dream location. So when Ben suggested tagging our nuptials on to our December trip to the Big Apple, it just made sense.

Within three weeks I had it all organised – the suits, the boots, the rings, photographer, limo for afterwards and, most importantly, the Humanist celebrant in Central Park. In fairness, I'd had the rings on standby since we'd started dating.

It was so cold on Christmas Day, minus fifteen, but Central Park was the perfect setting. Snow-capped avenues of trees blew in the wind under white clouds. Distant happy voices greeted each other with 'Merry Christmas', and the sound of carolers drifted through the air. We passed young lovers skating on the ice-rink, an old couple sharing a blanket in a horse and cart driven by Santa Claus, and there were even people crazy enough to be jogging in woolly hats. It was magical.

We'd been encouraged to write our vows beforehand, so everything would run smoothly, but we both thought it was more important to say what we wanted from the heart, unrehearsed. This was our Gretna Green, breaking away from the shackles and traditions, doing what we wanted to do.

The celebrant was hilarious. She must have been nudging ninety and spoke like the elderly Rose in the film *Titanic*, looking back on her life. At one point we wondered if she was going to get to the end of our ceremony alive. But as she went through the initial introductions and prepared for us to face one another for our vows, everything became calm. I took Ben's chilly hand in mine and placing a ring on the end of his finger, looked into his eyes.

'Ben, I will always love you, respect you, take care of you and be there for you no matter what. I will never let you down,' I told him earnestly. Over my frosty breath I could see his eyes brimming, smiling at me, as I pushed the ring down his finger. My heart was bursting. Then he took my hand and did the same.

'Richie, you have shown me what true love is. You have stayed beside me no matter what. Thank you for being all that you are and for wanting to share your life with me. I am truly grateful and love you with all my heart for now and forever.'

I tipped my head back to avoid my tears spilling over. The celebrant was beaming. 'Do you, Richie, take this man, to be your lawful wedded husband?'

'I do,' I choked.

'And do you, Ben, take this man to be your lawful wedded husband?'

'I do.'

'Well then,' the celebrant grinned, 'I now pronounce you – husband and husband – Mr & Mr Barlow.'

Possibly the best moment of my life.

We leaned into one another and sealed the deal with a kiss, Ben's warm lips a complete contrast to the outside air. A small crowd of passers-by stopped to cheer. It was surreal. Here we were, after such a rollercoaster of a start, proclaiming our love for each other for the rest of our lives. We'd entered this marriage with our eyes open, without secrets, and an understanding that this was just the beginning.

The photographer took us to a couple of key locations but it was so freezing we didn't get many shots. We were stomping our feet to keep the feeling in our toes, but the snapper was clearly more acclimatised to the New York temperatures than us.

'Could you look a bit less cold?' she kept saying to Ben.

I did my best to warm him up.

After the photos were done, we found a fabulous restaurant in the French Quarter and thawed out with succulent fillet steak cooked right at our table, swilled down with the best champagne.

It was perfect.

Richie – Who Cares?

We filled the rest of our trip with touristy stuff – saw the Statue of Liberty, went shopping to Macy's and hopped on the train to Philadelphia, which was an eye-opener. The weather was so bad that every time the train doors opened, snow blew in and settled. We had hot chocolate in Starbucks but struggled to stop ourselves from staring at some of the other customers. One woman was engaged in a very loud conversation on her mobile about the need to collect her methadone before picking her kids up from school. We didn't hang around.

When we arrived home, we decided to throw a belated festive bash at our house for all his family – to celebrate Christmas and our marriage. After my initial *faux pas* with Pam a couple of years earlier, I was mindful not to get too giddy. Fortunately, I'd also had chance to meet his brothers and Nana in the interim but knew my shaky start with Ben had left some of his family feeling sceptical.

We laid on some food and drink and everyone seemed in good spirits. His family were in my home. Our home. I circulated and chatted away about New York and our plans for the future, feeling naturally drawn to Ben's lovely Nana. I piled a few extra bits of food on her plate and sat with her as people got into the swing. Ben's brothers embraced me and welcomed me into the family with raised glasses instead of the raised eyebrows I'd been worrying about, and by the time everyone left, I was full of love.

Falling into bed, Ben turned to me and told me what his Auntie Pam had said after pulling him to one side.

'We take our family relationships for granted, don't we Ben?' she said, 'But for Richie this must be so strange just seeing us all getting along, joking around and enjoying each other's company.'

She'd hit the nail on the head, and it was such a relief to know I was understood. That one comment meant so much to me. It took his mum a little longer to warm to 'us' though, but that's because she'd seen how badly Ben had been treated by his ex for all those years – and I get that. Now, she fully accepts me and shows me the greatest respect. For my birthday a couple of years ago, his Nana sent me a special card with 'Grandson' on the front, which I will treasure forever.

23

•

Nightmares and Justice

LIFE CONTINUED apace. My business was growing and after a lot of discussion, Ben decided to join the company too. We fell into a happy pattern at home. I cherished the little things we did together, like having a cup of tea in bed in the morning or sharing an evening meal. The people in my life loved Ben and could see how he brought out the best in me. But my nightmares still wouldn't go away. I couldn't control what my brain was doing once I switched off, and I was haunted by situations from my past.

It was worrying Ben as much as me and he wanted to help me do something about it. He knew that other than the play therapy I'd had with Anna when I was a young boy, I'd never engaged with counselling, so he began looking into it on my behalf. All this coincided with the news in October 2017 about Harvey Weinstein, the Hollywood film producer, who was accused by various women in the industry of rape and sexual assault.

There was something about his case that I was drawn to. I looked at those victims on TV and social media who'd been brave enough to step forward and share their stories. It wasn't just what Weinstein had done, but the way he'd gone about it too, using his power and influence to coerce and gaslight vulnerable women and girls into feeling they had no other options for success.

The #MeToo movement took hold. It was originally spawned in 2006 after an online post by an activist called Tarana Burke. She'd been a Youth Camp worker and shared a story of how a young girl had been brave enough to open up to her about her mother's abusive boyfriend – but Tarana couldn't cope with hearing about it and sent the girl to someone else instead. As a result of Tarana's soul-searching afterwards, she launched the campaign to help build a network of women who could empathise with survivors of abuse.

When the Weinstein news broke over ten years later, actress Alyssa Milano helped #MeToo go viral with a tweet asking people who'd been harassed or assaulted to reply, to give others a sense of the magnitude of the problem. Women and men from all over the world did and dared to share their experiences – for many of them, it was the first time they'd spoken out.

The whole thing threw up so many repressed thoughts and feelings for me. I'd be walking the dogs and suddenly have a flashback to being cornered by Brett in the bushes at Farmlands. Or I might be in a lift and start shaking at the memory of meeting the pimp for the first time when I was just nine years old. I'd take a dirty plate to the sink and my throat would tighten at the sight of the washing up liquid bottle. I couldn't stop the images in my mind. It was like the genie had escaped and I couldn't push it back in.

As the momentum of the #MeToo movement grew, I noticed on Twitter that one of my favourite *Star Trek* actors, Anthony Rapp, had opened up about an incident with Kevin Spacey. He alleged Spacey had taken advantage of him in 1986, when Anthony was only fourteen years old.

I'd already been following Anthony on Twitter for a while, because not only is he a *Star Trek* actor, but his character, Lt. Paul Stamets is LGBT+. I just found him so inspiring and had already messaged him before his announcement about Spacey to tell him as much. But when Anthony publicly shared his story, it was a moment that just hit me.

Here was someone completely on my wavelength who'd gone through abuse too. The way he talked about the control and manipulation side of things rang so true. He wanted to show other people that you don't have to put up with it and sit quietly, that you can take the abuser's control away by telling the truth and seeking justice. It was Anthony's bravery at speaking out which ultimately gave me the courage to try to do the same. I just didn't know how or where to start.

Ben could sense I desperately needed to put my thoughts in order. He understood how important it was for me to start telling people about what really happened while I was growing up. Until I did that, there would be no closure. Ben also knew how traumatic this could potentially be for me, so wanted to find the right support. After a lot of searching, he came across The Truth Project on Facebook and tagged me in.

When I clicked on their website, I knew he'd found what I needed on the first page:

> The Truth Project gives victims and survivors of child sexual abuse the chance to put their experience on record. The Independent Inquiry into Child Sexual Abuse, chaired by Professor Alexis Jay OBE, was set up because of serious concerns that some organisations had failed and were continuing to fail to protect children from sexual abuse. Our remit is huge, but as a statutory inquiry we have unique authority to address issues that have persisted despite previous inquiries and attempts at reform.

This was it. My starting point.

I got in touch with them and was invited to share my story. It all happened in a building in a business park near Darlington. Ben came with me, obviously, and in the car on the way there, we wondered what the meeting might hold and if The Truth Project really could be what we were looking for.

Parking up we noticed the building looked pretty uninspiring, but Ben grabbed my hand, and we made our way through the double doors to the reception area. We gave our names to the woman behind the desk, and she asked us to take a seat, saying someone would be with us shortly.

A friendly looking guy approached.

'Richie Barlow?' he asked, looking between Ben and me.

'I'm Richie, yes,' I said, standing up.

Before I could say anything else, Ben was right in there, shaking his hand and letting this guy know what he was expecting.

'I want some counselling and compensation for what happened to my husband when he was growing up. I want an apology, and for someone to be held to account. Someone needs to say: *'We failed you, we're sorry.'*

He was braver than me and to be honest, it wasn't about the money. The guy looked a bit taken aback – he was one of the facilitators, but he reassured both of us that he'd do everything in his power to help. He suggested I follow him through to another office.

The facilitator was joined by an assistant facilitator, who was there to take notes. I was encouraged to tell them everything, right from the very beginning. I was hesitant at first, not really knowing where to start, but once I got going, that was it. It took a good few hours, but by the end of it, they had a potted version of my life so far. I told them about my mother's abuse, what I endured whilst in care at Willowdene and Farmlands, the incident at Aycliffe and subsequent coercion into prostitution by Phil.

I felt believed and understood. My story was going to be on record and my experiences would be used to help government and organisations know more about how they can better protect children in the future. It felt good to share what I'd been through, and it was reassuring to know that other people were talking about their experiences too.

But it threw up the fact that I if I wanted justice, I needed evidence to back up my stories, so I set about trying to find my personal records from when I was in the care of Nottinghamshire County Council. It was important to me to read those records, to see where I'd been failed. I wanted to know why those in charge hadn't done more to protect me, when they clearly knew that between the ages of nine and fourteen years old, I'd been caught up in some serious sexual abuse. I also needed to see, in black and white, what my mother's reasoning was for dumping me into that system in the first place.

Trying to get anything out of the council is nigh on

impossible – particularly if it involves them having to admit to mistakes. After a few frustrating months of drawing a blank, I contacted The Truth Project again, who put me in touch with a solicitor called Debbie, from Instalaw. The Truth Project also arranged for me to have a twenty-session block of counselling, paid for by Durham County Council. While Debbie set to work finding all the relevant documents, I began opening up even more.

My counselling sessions were with a lovely woman who made me feel comfortable immediately. I prefer talking to women in general, so perhaps that was part of it, but whatever the reason, she was brilliant. She listened properly and gave me points of reference which really helped. I had a lot of epiphany moments as buried memories resurfaced and we dealt with them one by one.

After each session, I felt a bit lighter, more comfortable, like I understood myself a little more. She taught me to look at things in a different way, not as that little child anymore, but as an adult. That was a game-changer. It made me see the bigger picture and understand that what happened to me was through other people's actions beyond my control. Ben had repeatedly told me that none of it was my fault and I wanted to believe him, but it was the counsellor who truly made me see it. I shed a lot of tears with her.

I was learning to use the tools needed to process trauma. It was like taking a situation out of a box, looking at it through adult's eyes, then throwing away all the negative emotions associated with it, understanding that the people perpetrating that trauma couldn't hurt me anymore. It was about accepting that I will never forget, but that I don't need to hide from or be fearful of the past.

'Are you okay listening to this?' I kept asking her.

'I am,' she said, and told me how counsellors get their own counselling debriefs to help them deal with upsetting stories.

There was a point when what I was discussing could be used as evidence, so I was reminded that it was being documented in case it was ever needed in court.

Meanwhile, my solicitor Debbie had managed to get her hands on boxes of folders documenting my time in care at Farmlands. Unfortunately, it was harder to unearth much paperwork from the previous children's home, Willowdene, but what she did have, she went through with a fine toothcomb and summarised it into key events.

The summary itself was ten pages long and made for extremely difficult reading. There are so many instances when I was clearly in need of adult care and intervention, yet none had been forthcoming. The number of times I absconded was unbelievable – but the reports insinuated that I was running away because I was trying to cause trouble. There seemed to have been very few attempts to address the root cause of the problem. I couldn't believe they hadn't placed me on the child protection register.

Any sane, caring adult working in the social care sector would have seen my behaviour as an obvious response to trauma.

As Gary says, social workers are trained not to take behaviours at face value, but to look for reasons as to why a child might be acting that way, then help them. It is their job to do that. The summary is a catalogue of missed opportunities at the hands of lazy staff in a care system where that was the farthest thing from some of their minds.

Debbie felt we had a watertight case to get some form of justice from Nottinghamshire County Council, and on 11th December 2018 she wrote to them, detailing evidence to back up the claims. It took the council almost a year to write this letter back, using the fact that my mother had placed me in care of her own volition, rather than the council insisting I was removed from her, as a way of denying responsibility.

On 9th October 2019, Debbie received this letter:

RB v Nottinghamshire County Council
We write further in this matter and to confirm our repudiation of the claim.

We refer to your initial letter dated 11 December 2018 (herein referred to as 'the letter'). You allege that your client suffered personal injury arising out of sexual abuse suffered during his childhood whilst living in the care of Nottinghamshire County Council. You consider that Nottinghamshire County Council is liable in negligence for failing to adequately protect and promote your client's safety, welfare and wellbeing.

Having investigated the matter, our position is that your client was at all times **voluntarily** accommodated pursuant to Section 20 of the Children's Act 1989, both at Willowdene Children's Home and at Farmland's Children's Home, before moving onto a secure unit in Newton Aycliffe, County Durham. The letter states that your client had been taken into care prior to his first placement at Willowdene, but that is incorrect; there was no care order.

As you will be well aware, the Supreme Court recently held in CN & GN v Poole Borough Council [2019] UKSC 25 that as a general rule, local authorities do not owe a duty of care of children to protect them from harm caused by others. There is an exception to that general rule where there is a Care Order, but that is not the case here. The harm complained of at Willowdene and Farmlands relates to alleged abuse by others. It follows that if there is no duty of care, there can be no question of any breach of duty.

We would add that even if there were a duty of care owed, it would not have been breached. The alleged abuse is by either your client's peers, or by members of the public **with whom your client sought contact**. Your client positively rejected assistance by both the police and our client at the time.

Yours faithfully,
Weightmans LLP

To say that was a kick in the teeth is a bit of an understatement. If the council weren't responsible for me, who was? And to suggest that I sought contact with my abusers was frankly insane. As if any child would choose to endure that, if an option of a safe, loving home had been provided.

As a child, I had clearly been in a lose-lose situation, and nobody stepped in to save me. It's no exaggeration to say that on several occasions I could have died.

This wasn't the end of it. Debbie and I wanted to fight to the bitter end. I hadn't gone through all this for some person I didn't know to tell me that's just the way it was, that nobody was really to blame.

Richie – Who Cares?

As Debbie fought back on my behalf, I decided it was also time for me to speak to the police about my experiences with Phil and how, due to my vulnerable childhood, he managed to coerce me into prostitution and dupe me into a load of debt in my early twenties.

The police did listen. They were respectful and took a record of everything I said, but it never went anywhere. There were no convictions or even cautions, but I know what he did as well as he does. There was one good thing to come out of telling the police though, and that was their referral of me back to The Truth Project, where they arranged more counselling. I was offered another twenty sessions to deal with the Phil trauma, which helped to a certain extent.

Because I understood the counselling process now, I approached these next sessions without holding back and was looking forward to getting a lot off my chest. But before I had chance to get to my first appointment, the whole country went into lockdown due to the Coronavirus pandemic. It was a blow on many levels, but my main concern was the safety of Ben, our family and friends.

The Dog Walker business became more difficult because many of my customers were now either furloughed or working from home, so were more on hand for their pets and glad for the change of scenery a walk afforded them. I received minimal financial help from the government, making things extremely tight as we lost income. It's only because I was savvy enough to save over the years that I could just about cushion the blow.

As people got used to different ways of working, I was offered my counselling sessions via zoom. It wasn't ideal but it was better than nothing and gave me a focus other than work. I talked about the abusive, toxic relationship with Phil and, as with my previous sessions, the more I shared, the better I felt. My sleeping habits improved, and my nightmares seemed less frequent or violent.

Despite having been perennially on the wrong side of the law, this enforced period of inactivity also gave me the chance to pursue something I'd been wanting to do for a long time – join the special police force. It was a role I could do on top of my Dog Walker work at just sixteen hours a month.

This wasn't the first time I'd applied though. My initial attempt was way back when I was living with Phil in Wetherby, after spotting a recruitment advert from West Yorkshire Police. I'd gone along to Wetherby police station and sat down with an officer, but as soon as I tried to explain about my criminal record, the conversation was cut short. He very coldly just told me he couldn't help me and that was that.

But now it was 2020. Time had passed, life had moved on and as far as I was concerned, I'd proven beyond a shadow of a doubt that I was a decent member of society. More than that, I was a living example of how a person can turn their life around irrespective of their horrific past. I applied online to be considered for a special constable role within North Yorkshire Police.

Things were looking hopeful. They'd received my application form and I was invited to attend various online meetings where I was set further tests to assess my skills, ability and resilience. I felt like I had a bit of an edge having already worked in the emergency services. They asked for examples of scenarios where I had helped others or used my skills to benefit those in need, and I had loads to draw on.

Then I got invited to a pre-interview session on zoom. There were just over fifty potential recruits logged on to that event, where a group of police officers and the Chief Constable told us more about the volunteer role and how to approach the next stage of the process. The opening line was 'Congratulations for getting this far. We're now going to prepare you for the interview.'

After that, they did Police National Computer checks on all the candidates, a central system holding information about individuals who have been reprimanded, cautioned, warned, arrested or convicted for a recordable offence. Then they emailed me to say *because of the custodial sentence that you received, we're going to have to terminate your application.*

But I had already explained in my initial application about that. I'd told them that I hadn't been sent to Aycliffe Young People's

Centre for punishment, I had been placed there for my own protection and there had been a miscarriage of justice.

The senior police officer in charge of this application was also critical about my activity on social media. I already had friends in the police force and through my Twitter account, I ended up connecting with a lot more. He said that I'd used Twitter to try and pursue a career in the force. It felt to me like he was using his own personal views to attack my integrity and I found that hurtful and unprofessional.

I appealed their decision to terminate my application, but they said the only way I would have a chance of a success with them in the future would be if I had my conviction overturned. It was galling and yet another reminder of how I'd been monumentally let down by the authorities when I was growing up.

It all came back to the same thing – my mother. If she hadn't been so cruel, lying about the abuse of my sister, I might not have been dragged into that particular abyss where not enough people cared about keeping me safe from physical, sexual and psychological abuse.

But I refuse to be defined by events in my past which were out of my control, and I am currently looking into the possibility of having that conviction overturned.

24

•

Resolution

ON 4th OCTOBER 2020, Ben was driving between customers, listening to BBC Radio 4. But when the presenter introduced their *Desert Island Discs* feature, he found a safe place to pull over and rang me straight away. The guest that day was actress Samantha Morton, whom he knew had spent some of her childhood in the care system in Nottingham.

'Richie, get Radio 4 on, now,' he said. 'It's Samantha Morton and I think she might talk about the same place your brother was taken to.'

I was about to set off for my next job too, so jumped in the van and tuned in. Samantha's story made my hair stand on end. I was totally immersed, I felt like I had a sister on the radio, talking about our shared experiences in care. She'd spent a lot of time at Red Tiles children's home where Luke stayed and had witnessed abuse herself. She'd even threatened to kill one of the older kids who was exploiting one of the youngsters. I felt she'd have stuck up for me too.

Her words proved to me that sexual exploitation in Nottinghamshire children's homes was endemic long before I went to Willowdene. It sounded like there was already someone in a children's home not far from Farmlands, involved in prostituting children as young as eight or nine years old.

She solidified everything I'd been thinking about Nottinghamshire County Council. This was someone else –

someone who people listened to – telling the world how it was. I wasn't making any of it up and neither was she. It was also the first time that I'd heard of somebody else brought up in care who was doing well for themselves. I'd seen her in all sorts on TV and loved the film *Minority Report,* but had no idea what she'd been through. I felt a stupid pride in her achievements and found myself shouting 'Get in, you've done it' at the radio.

Less than four months later, on 17th February 2021, my solicitor Debbie got in touch with me again. She had details of an out of court compensation settlement and a letter of apology from Nottinghamshire County Council.

I rushed to agree to the settlement as it came at a time when Ben and I needed the money due to the pandemic. Had we been in a better financial position at the time, I think we might have held out for something better. Or I might have treated us to a new car.

For my lost childhood I was awarded forty thousand pounds. There were solicitor's fees to pay out of that too, so all told, for everything, I received the equivalent of a near minimum wage annual salary, and this letter:

Dear Mr Barlow

I write in my role as the Corporate Director for Nottinghamshire County Council Children's Services and on behalf of the Council. My purpose in writing is to apologise to you for the abuse you experienced as a child while in our care. You entered into the care system at a young age, and you should have been safe from harm and it is clear that this was not the case and I am truly and sincerely sorry for that.

Locally support services for adults have developed over recent years to try and ensure that individual needs can be met, including for those who suffered abuse while in public care. I am enclosing some information for you about those support services in case this might be something that you feel could be of help or interest to you.

Yours sincerely
Nottinghamshire County Council.

That was it. Two paragraphs all told. Should I pursue it further? Is that enough for everything I went through?

The letter is important because it is an admission of lack of care – and that's what I was after, but some of my family and friends don't think it's worth the paper it's printed on.

In my heart though, I know that no words or amount of recompense could make it better. What happened won't go away. It is a part of my life, of what and who I am.

But I am only one person in that whole wretched care system. Imagine how many more boys and girls there were, just like me, going through hell, silenced by adults, frightened, hurt, abused and alone. If they're reading this, I hope they too find the courage to tell their stories and seek justice, because the only way to break the cycle and find a sense of calm is by speaking out.

And I feel like I've only just begun.

Yes, I have the apology from Nottinghamshire County Council. But I'm not done with the way I was treated by the police regarding the caution when I was at Farmlands. That officer in the interview room did not follow up what I'd told him about being forced into prostitution. He did not do his job. If he had, there's a possibility I would never have ended up enmeshed in the whole situation of the fire with Brett – because he might have been removed from Farmlands or I might have been moved to a different children's home away from him.

And what about justice for being raped while at Aycliffe Young People's Centre? At the time, I had neither the will or nouse to fight the staff or authorities at Durham County Council about that. I was coerced into accepting their explanation of there being no point in pursuing it because it wouldn't change the sentence of the perpetrator. As I see this in black and white, I find it even harder to believe. What about the victim? How is being told to forget about being raped in any way justice? I was basically blocked from seeking help from the police.

There are still so many loose ends to tie up, but I can't let them dominate my life and spoil what I have now. I think I've earned the right to enjoy some peace with my husband. He feels like my reward, my ultimate prize, like karma finally found a way to rebalance the trauma by gifting him to me.

I know he will be by my side throughout the next chapter, however that might pan out. If I reach for his hand in the middle of the night, he is all the reassurance I need.

He is there. I am safe. I am loved.

Epilogue

Aycliffe Young Peoples Centre, 1997,
with my foster mother, Anna Daiches

DURING THE course of putting this book together, I have reconnected with my foster mum, Anna Daiches, on a much deeper and wider level. I have re-met some of her extended family – cousins, nieces, her brother and her Auntie (Jenni Calder, the Scottish literary historian and author of twenty-eight books).

Anna's family are spread far and wide, but Ben and I made the trip to Scotland to spend some time with them all at the end of 2021. It was amazing. I felt like I just belonged and they opened their arms to me as if I was a long-lost son.

As far as Anna is concerned, I *am* her son. It says in my records from Farmlands that a Scottish family were in the process of trying to adopt me – Anna's family, but it fell through because I was sent to Aycliffe Young People's centre. Anna wants to set that straight and recently she asked if she could look into adopting me as an adult. I'm sure you can imagine how emotional I was at her offer.

In some countries, in some circumstances, it is possible to adopt an adult (USA, Canada, Japan and Germany to name a few).

Unfortunately, in the UK, it is still illegal to be adopted once a person reaches the age of eighteen years old. However, I have had a meeting with the Corporate Director for Children, Families and Cultural Services at Nottinghamshire County Council and he is right behind me. He has linked me up with a campaigner at a charity called Become for young people in care and care leavers, in the hope that there may be a way forward with mine and Anna's wishes.

Although the main reason for getting adopted as an adult is so that I can genuinely say I have a mum, one other factor to consider is inheritance. As it stands, if Ben and I ended up dying together, my birth family would be able to contest my will in the hope of laying claim to my estate. That is the absolute last thing I would ever wish. If Anna was legally my mum, I know everything would be dealt with as per my wishes.

It could be a long journey, but Anna and I are hoping that eventually, we might be able to somehow affect a change in UK Law so that we can officially become mother and son.

In a dream scenario, that law would be called 'Richie's Law'.

Alison Moyet
@AlisonMoyet

Replying to @roddenberry @The_DogWalker and @Madonna

There are days we feel pointless & a drain on all. I fell upon this message of yours and found todays redemption. Thank you for keeping me in your bones. I am tremendously proud that you did. Thank you for my place. Formidable you xx

12:27 · 28/04/2022 · Twitter for iPhone